THE **BEST**

LOS ANGELES

SPORTS

ARGUMENTS

THE **100** MOST
CONTROVERSIAL, DEBATABLE
QUESTIONS FOR DIE-HARD
FANS

J.A. ADANDE

SOURCEBOOKS, INC.®
NAPERVILLE, ILLINOIS

$1

D0372395

© 2007 by J.A. Adande

Cover and internal design © 2007 by Sourcebooks, Inc.

Photo page 291 courtesy of Robert Gould

Sourcebooks and the colophon are registered trademarks of Sourcebooks, Inc.

All rights reserved. No part of this book may be reproduced in any form or by any electronic or mechanical means including information storage and retrieval systems—except in the case of brief quotations embodied in critical articles or reviews—without permission in writing from its publisher, Sourcebooks, Inc.

All team names, brand names, and product names used in this book are trademarks, registered trademarks, or trade names of their respective holders. Sourcebooks, Inc., is not associated with any product or vendor in this book.

Published by Sourcebooks, Inc.

P.O. Box 4410, Naperville, Illinois 60567-4410

(630) 961-3900

Fax: (630) 961-2168

www.sourcebooks.com

Library of Congress Cataloging-in-Publication Data

Adande, J. A.

  The best Los Angeles sports arguments : the 100 most controversial, debatable questions for die-hard fans / J.A. Adande.

    p. cm.

  Includes index.

  ISBN-13: 978-1-4022-1106-5 (pbk.)

  ISBN-10: 1-4022-1106-6 (pbk.)

  1. Sports—California—Los Angeles—Miscellanea. I. Title.

GV584.5.L7A43 2007

796.'0979494—dc22

                      2007029258

Printed and bound in the United States of America

CH 10 9 8 7 6 5 4 3 2 1

CONTENTS

THE BEST LOS ANGELES SPORTS ARGUMENTS

THE BEST LOS ANGELES SPORTS ARGUMENTS

INTRODUCTION

What got you hooked?

For me it was Magic Johnson as a rookie, running the fast break, dishing out no-look passes, celebrating every triumph big and small with hugs, high-fives, and that billboard-sized smile.

From that point, Los Angeles sports teams weren't just something to notice occasionally, such as when the Rams made it to the Super Bowl. Every game worked its way into the ebbs and flows of my life. People who knew me well could predict my mood on any given day based on whether or not the Lakers won the night before.

I spent many nights waiting for Chick Hearn to put a Lakers game in the refrigerator before turning off my bedside clock radio. I spent many summer afternoons listening to Vin Scully's masterful descriptions of "Dah-ger baseball" on a transistor radio on the beach.

Along with the rest of the city, I got swept up in Fernandomania. Then the Raiders arrived, and soon L.A. had a Super Bowl champion. The Olympics brought the world's greatest athletes to town for a two-week party. But it felt as if there was an athletic festival every year.

East Coasters complain that there's no change of seasons in Southern California. Sure there is. You can tell what time of year it is by which local team is in the play-offs. One April when I lived in Washington, D.C., I told a friend it was time to get excited because the NBA playoffs were starting. "Oh, yeah, I guess they are," he responded. It had been so long since the local team even reached the postseason that he never thought of April as being any different.

That's not the case in L.A. There's such an abundance of teams and such a demand for high quality that someone is always winning something. This is not a town defined by its losers, angst, or suffering. Out here, droughts are actually droughts, not stretches without championships. If you hear anyone talking about suffering through a long wait, they're probably talking about the line for a Dodger Dog.

We have been blessed with an abundance of athletic options. Dodgers and Angels. Lakers and Clippers. Ducks and Kings. UCLA and USC...

But for these pages, the keyword isn't "and." It's "or." Time to make the tough choices.

The Lakers or Dodgers as L.A.'s favorite team?

Wilt Chamberlain, Kareem Abdul-Jabbar, or Shaquille O'Neal as the Lakers' greatest center?

O. J. Simpson, Marcus Allen, or Reggie Bush as USC's greatest Heisman Trophy winner?

See, sometimes it's possible to have too much of a good thing—at least when it comes time to picking the superlatives among L.A.'s superstars.

Oh, there are piles of futility to sort through as well. Try choosing among classic Angels collapses or Clippers draft-day flubs.

Sports are fueled by speculation. We get definitive answers by way of scores and statistics, but those aren't what get us talking. If you tell your friend that Russell Martin went 2 for 4 last night, you'll get a nod and a quick comment. But if you say Martin will end up as a greater Dodger catcher than Mike Piazza—well, you'd better dig in for an argument.

You won't agree with every choice in this book. You're not supposed to. If every sports fan shared the same opinion, it would be too quiet. Stadiums are supposed to be filled with noise, and the time between games is supposed to be filled with conjecture.

Feel free to think of your own answers. Feel free to cheer or boo the ones provided here. But there's one thing we can agree about from the start: When it comes to Los Angeles sports, there's no shortage of material to debate.

IT'S AN L.A. THING

IS LOS ANGELES A GREAT SPORTS TOWN?

1 It's a shame the question even has to be asked, but years of sniping fans and media types across the country criticizing the local population's sports passion and mocking the lack of an NFL team have given Los Angeles a bad rap.

There's the tired cliché of fans arriving late and leaving early, obviously put forth by people who have never tried to drive on Interstate 5 in rush hour. There's the accusation that the famous and wannabe famous come to be seen, not heard.

But anyone who reduces the Los Angeles sports scene to those old saws never stood in the old Forum when it was "Showtime," or heard the buzz of anticipation when Eric Gagne charged out of the bullpen at Dodger Stadium.

Sports are entertainment. And in the showbiz capital of the world, the people who spend their working hours producing entertainment deserve to be entertained in their own free time. Athletes who were lucky enough to be here—the ones who really got it—knew that they weren't just players, they were performers.

And what performances we've seen, and created. The greatest are either from here or come here. At one time, football's single-season rushing record, basketball's all-time scoring and assists records, and hockey's all-time goals record were all set by players wearing Los Angeles uniforms.

It's a city where it was possible to watch Bo Jackson play for the Raiders in the afternoon and see Magic Johnson in person in the evening. How many towns offered something like that?

In 1988–89, Magic won the NBA MVP award while Wayne Gretzky captured the NHL's Hart Trophy. Both played at the Forum, marking the first time a single building was home to the MVPs of hockey and basketball simultaneously.

They're part of a list of legends that includes eight Heisman Trophy winners, seven NBA MVPs, three Wooden Award winners, two NFL MVPs, and an NHL Hart Trophy winner.

Put a good, entertaining product out there and this city will support it. And it seems the fans' appetite for sports is more voracious than ever. In 2006, the Angels and Dodgers each drew more than 3.4 million fans. The Lakers and the Clippers (who had the best season in franchise history) each drew more than 18,000 per game to Staples Center. The USC Trojans set a Pacific-10 Conference attendance record.

For those who can't be there in person, the broadcasters who bring you the action are the best in the business. Los Angeles has been blessed with Hall of Fame announcers

3

Vin Scully and Jaime Jarrin on the Dodgers and Bob Miller on the Kings. Dick Emberg got his start out here. And of course, any time you hear a basketball announcer use a phrase such as *airball* or *finger roll*, they're taking words out of the basketball dictionary created by the late Chick Hearn, the longtime voice of the Lakers.

Even the best announcers need good material to work with, and traditionally the product has been top-notch. It has to be to get attention in this city. (For purposes of this book, we're annexing Orange County. If the Angels of Anaheim can take the Los Angeles name for marketing reasons, we can claim the O.C. to strengthen our arguments.)

Since 1984, local teams have won at least one Super Bowl, World Series, NBA championship, Stanley Cup, NCAA football championship, and NCAA basketball championship.

No other city can claim trophies in all of those sports during that time. Los Angeles holds that sole distinction even though it hasn't had an NFL entry since the 1994 season. But even the lack of a local team can be a bonus. Instead of getting stuck with a bad game on Sunday—or even worse, a blackout because the home game didn't sell out—the L.A. airwaves are cleared for the best network game of the week.

See, there are benefits to not having a team. But since that's such a lingering issue, we might as well get to it now....

WHO IS TO BLAME FOR THE NFL NOT HAVING A TEAM IN LOS ANGELES?

 This is a story in which there are no heroes, only a cast of characters filled with flaws . . . kind of like *The Sopranos*, only without the whackings.

The Rams had been in Los Angeles since moving from Cleveland in 1946. The Raiders had only been in town since 1982, but they gave the city its first Super Bowl victory in 1984. So who's to blame for their leaving?

We'll start with the owners, the Raiders' Al Davis and the Rams' Georgia Frontiere. The Raiders were stuck in an antiquated stadium, sorely lacking in luxury suites. The Rams were losing $6 million to $7 million annually. But this is one of those times that sports goes beyond business and enters the realm of civic responsibility. There might have been economic hardships, but how many other private businesses expect the city to guarantee profits? Any other enterprise would not feel entitled to finishing in the black.

What about the community? The economists say that the benefits a sports team provides to a city are more psychological than financial. Teams unify the population and winning teams fill the citizens with a sense of pride—almost as if the people themselves accomplished something.

None of that came into account with the Rams and the Raiders. This was all about dollars. From a fiscal standpoint, moving made sense. St. Louis did everything but pay for the Rams' new company stationery. The city offered a new stadium, built the Rams a practice facility, and let them keep the luxury suite and concession revenues. While the deal the Raiders received from Oakland wasn't quite as sweet, the Raiders did get a ticket purchase guarantee from the city and $100 million in renovations for the Oakland–Alameda County Coliseum.

The fans didn't do much to help. An average of 42,312 per game showed up during the Rams' last season in Anaheim, some 20,000 fewer than their first season there. And for the very last game, with the move looming, attendance was at an all-time low of 25,705. As statements go, it was more "Bon voyage" than "Please don't leave us."

"Maybe if they had reacted sooner, and with some passion and tried to find a way," Frontiere told the *Los Angeles Times*. "But it wasn't like that. It was like, 'Oh well, let them go.'"

Then again, maybe if the Rams had reacted sooner and put a good team on the field, attendance wouldn't have been so dismal. But it was like, "Oh well, let them pay to watch junky teams."

The Rams had losing records in their final five seasons in Anaheim, and they traded star running back Eric Dickerson in the midst of a Hall of Fame career. (He rushed for 1,659 yards and 14 touchdowns the next year, his first full season as an Indianapolis Colt.)

The Raiders didn't have a losing record, and they didn't have a huge financial windfall awaiting them. Their move might have simply been a matter of Al Davis' impatience. The owners of the Hollywood Park racetrack wanted to build a new stadium for him on their property in Inglewood, but Davis didn't want to spend two more years in the Coliseum while the new property was being built. He also wanted monetary guarantees from the league and Hollywood Park.

The Raiders fans were consistently enthusiastic, and constantly intimidating to opposing fans. But they weren't constantly in the seats on Sundays. The Coliseum was only half-filled in the Raiders' final season in Los Angeles. And while the numbers decreased, it just meant the arrest-per-1,000 fans ratio increased. In many ways, the fans' behavior kept more fans from showing up, depriving all of the fans.

Where was the commissioner? The departure of the two teams from Los Angeles and the failure to replace them loom as the two biggest holes in Paul Tagliabue's 17-year tenure. They certainly weren't the only moves—there was relatively rampant "franchise free agency" on his watch, as the St. Louis Cardinals, the Houston Oilers, and the original Cleveland Browns all moved.

In the case of the Raiders, Tagliabue had to be wary of getting entangled in a legal battle. Davis successfully sued the league and won the right to move to Los Angeles from Oakland during the reign of Pete Rozelle, Tagliabue's predecessor.

But it's worth noting that after the Raiders and Rams left, Tagliabue did flex strongly enough to keep the Tampa Bay Buccaneers and Seattle Seahawks from moving to L.A. Tagliabue got word that the Buccaneers were talking to the Hollywood Park people and put a halt to it. In the Seahawks' case, owner Ken Behring had actually moved the team down to the Rams' old training complex and was ready to start practices when the league told him to pack up and head back to Seattle. In both cases the teams were threatened with $500,000 fines.

Money seemed to get their attention. Tagliabue would know that nothing catches an NFL owner's eyes like dollar bills. That green paper is certainly much sexier than market-size figures. You would think, in the interest of the league's long-term growth, it would be more important to be in the nation's second-largest market, instead of the 10th (Houston) or 21st (St. Louis). But the NFL was thinking short-term.

Ultimately, it was Houstonian Bob McNair's willingness to pony up a $700 million expansion fee that beat out the best bid by a makeshift coalition made up of real estate magnate Ed Roski and Hollywood mogul Michael Ovitz, who had ditched his efforts to put a stadium in Carson and joined the Coliseum crowd. The biggest check won. The end.

In some ways Los Angeles is more useful to the NFL as a perpetual suitor. That helped fuel the stadium race that saw a construction boom of 17 stadiums during Tagliabue's tenure. As long as the Coliseum and the Rose Bowl were empty on Sundays, teams could always use the threat of moving to Los Angeles to coerce their local governments into building a new stadium, too—or to drive up bidding for an expansion franchise.

That seemed to be the only use Tagliabue had for the Coliseum. The NFL didn't like the old building and wasn't enamored with the neighborhood. Baltimore Ravens owner Art Modell provided the most colorful description of the league's attitude toward a renovated Coliseum when he told reporters at the owners meetings: "Trying to put a new dress on an old hooker is not the way I want to go dancing."

And yet the Coliseum Commission and its backers in the City Council kept re-applying the lipstick, trying to attract a suitor. That's why they, more than anyone else, get the blame for the city's exclusion from the NFL club.

Just about everyone who has dealt with the Coliseum Commission left, usually on bad terms. The Rams, the first major professional tenant, fled to Anaheim in 1980. UCLA took its football team to the Rose Bowl. In the 1960s, a fed-up Jack Kent Cooke left the adjacent Sports Arena and built the Forum to house his Lakers—just to spite a Coliseum Commissioner who literally laughed in his face when he threatened to do it, Cooke later claimed. And the Raiders left when Davis felt the Coliseum wouldn't be able to provide the necessary amenities in the changing NFL stadium game. (Since the commission spent $100 million making repairs and safety improvements to the stadium following the 1994 Northridge earthquake, it was not about to whip out the checkbook again.)

Even after its pro tenants had left, the Coliseum Commission kept popping up in places, like the unwelcome relative who shows up at the doorstep, bags in hand. When Peter O'Malley still owned the Dodgers, he envisioned building a football stadium next to his baseball palace in Chavez Ravine. Then the City Council told him to cool out and leave the NFL business to the Coliseum. Phil Anschutz, one of the country's wealthiest men and the main money behind Staples Center and the Home Depot Center, took a few exploratory steps toward landing an NFL team. However, he'd only do it if he could be assured of a hassle-free process. But the Coliseum Commission let it be known it was willing to spend $1 million to explore NFL possibilities, and that was enough to scare off Anschutz. No one with that amount of money has stepped forward since.

The Coliseum Commission has somehow managed to remain in the game, long after the Dodger Stadium option was gone, after the Carson bid was dropped, and after Pasadena's City Council cooled off on the Rose Bowl. Of course, the Coliseum hasn't had a strong financial backer lined up or a team ready to move there. It's always been short on solutions, long on problems.

WILL THE NFL RETURN TO LOS ANGELES?

3 Most of the arguments for the NFL coming back are emotional or sentimental. It starts with the city's ego. It just doesn't feel right to have smaller burgs such as Charlotte, St. Louis, or Green Bay in the exclusive NFL club while Los Angeles sits outside. It is the nation's top sport, and somehow the second-largest city has not been deemed worthy.

The better argument for putting a team in Los Angeles is an appeal to the tourist in every member of the NFL family. Having an NFL team in L.A. would mean the league could bring the Super Bowl back to L.A. The annual carnival of corporate sponsorship, with its hordes of visitors on expense accounts, is the NFL's reward not only to the most fortunate cities within its realm, but also a treat for the league itself. It's an excuse to get out of the office and head to some desirable locale for a week—as if the Pro Bowl game in Hawaii or annual off-season meetings weren't nice enough.

What would be a better place to spend a week in early February than Los Angeles? While snow covers the ground of most of the country, the average February temperature in L.A. is 70 degrees. Some of the greatest chefs in the country create innovative menus for the city's restaurants. Visitors can mingle with the eclectic characters on the Venice Boardwalk, take a trip through Hollywood history on the Walk of Fame, or party with celebrities at the hot nightspots (provided they can get past the velvet rope).

Few cities can meet the NFL's standards for climate, stadium size, and hotel capacity in order to host a Super Bowl. And it seems that every time a new candidate pops up—such as Dallas, thanks to its new billion-dollar stadium—another potential host city drops off. New Orleans, once a steady part of the Super Bowl rotation, must show that it can be a viable candidate again after being devastated by Hurricane Katrina. San Diego has been a great host for three Super Bowls, but the NFL has now vowed to stay away unless the Chargers get a new stadium.

Los Angeles and the Super Bowl have a long and successful history together. The Coliseum hosted the first matchup of the NFL and the old American Football League at the Coliseum in 1967, and L.A. has hosted seven Super Bowls, including five games at the Rose Bowl in Pasadena. It would be like reuniting with a lost friend.

It's no surprise that the back-to-Los Angeles movement seemed to gain momentum when the league suffered through Super Bowl weeks in unprepared Jacksonville and snowy Detroit in 2005 and 2006. Sometimes it's an up-close look at the rest of the dating pool that sends you running back to the arms of your ex.

But that's an emotional response. The NFL always gets back to the cold numbers. And the digits don't add up in Los Angeles' favor.

First of all, things would be much simpler if L.A. could keep the number of possible sites for a team at one. There could be a unified approach, a single voice speaking to the league, and no diffusion of attention or funding. Instead, there always seem to be multiple sites vying for attention, be it the Coliseum, Anaheim, or the Rose Bowl in Pasadena. The league can play each contestant against each other, forcing concessions or more expenditures and ultimately making any effort to land a team even more costly.

Then there's the number 32. Right now the NFL has balance, with eight divisions of four teams each, and every team can play during weeks with a full schedule. To add an expansion team would throw the schedule out of whack— not to mention bring in another owner to dilute the share each team takes from the league's pot. Not even the prospect of a quick jolt of cash from an expansion fee (probably half a billion dollars or more) seems to be enough to convince owners to take in any new members.

So that means relocation. The only reason for a team to leave its current city is because the local government won't give it a new stadium. Only the Minnesota Vikings, San Diego Chargers, San Francisco 49ers, and New Orleans Saints are playing in outdated stadiums that could prompt a move. The problem is, Los Angeles politicians have never indicated that they're eager to commit hundreds of millions of dollars to building a stadium.

In almost any other pro sport, it might be worth it for an owner to move to Los Angeles and spend his own money on a stadium, reaping the benefits of being in a major market. But with the NFL's revenue-sharing policies, there is no such incentive. There's only one central television contract, not the individual deals that boost the local revenues of Major League Baseball and NBA teams. Ticket revenues are shared as well. Why spend the money just so everyone else can benefit?

And how much money would it cost? Some estimates have placed the cost of a new stadium in the Los Angeles area at $1 billion. And if someone had to buy a team from a current owner in order to move it here, that could tack on an extra $500 million.

There are some potential benefits to various locations: the state of California could promise infrastructure improvements for the area around the Coliseum, and Anaheim could provide financial incentives to build in a business zone near Angel Stadium. But no one ever stood up and said, "I have $1.5 billion that I'm ready to spend on a team and a stadium."

That would have grabbed the NFL's attention. Instead, there has been silence, and the NFL moved on, always looking for the bigger, better deal. The cost of getting here will only continue to increase, which means the chances of it actually happening will continue to decrease.

15

At Super Bowl XLI, discussion of a team wasn't just moved to the back burner. It wasn't even in the kitchen.

SO WHOSE TOWN IS IT?

 Even when the NFL *was* here, the Dodgers and Lakers still had a greater connection with the city. The Rams arrived first, in 1946, but back then the NFL wasn't the monster that it became in the 1960s.

And by the time the NFL did take off, the Dodgers had already established themselves as the bigger—and better—team.

The Dodgers moved from Brooklyn after the 1957 season, then played the first game in their temporary home at the Coliseum on April 18, 1958. The next year, they won the World Series, beating the Chicago White Sox in six games. After two years in the big leagues, L.A. already had a champion.

More than that, it had legitimacy. Baseball still ruled the sports world at that time, and now Los Angeles had a team to call its own. Soon the Dodgers had a majestic home when they moved into their new stadium in Chavez Ravine in 1962.

As the great Jim Murray described opening day at the new ballpark: "In a funny way, it was the day when L.A. was certified as a major player in the complex of American cities—no longer just the place where Charlie Chaplin waved his cane, Pauline had her perils, and the cowboys and Indians chased each other down Gower Gulch while a director shouted 'Action!' No longer just Flicker City. Goodbye Tinseltown."

The Dodgers won two more championships in 1963 and 1965, featuring stars such as Sandy Koufax, Don Drysdale, Willie Davis, and Maury Wills.

It was a love affair. In 1959 the Dodgers became the second major league franchise to ever draw 2 million fans in a season. In 1978 they became the first to draw 3 million. By then they had become a long-term institution in a city with a short-term memory.

But it's also a town that likes to go with the hot new thing, and the very next year the hot thing was wearing a Lakers uniform. Magic Johnson came to Los Angeles in 1979, dazzled everyone with his big smile and no-look passes, and won a championship as a rookie. He would win four more championships before he was done. The Lakers made appearances in the NBA finals on an almost annual basis, and in the process, they changed the sports culture of the town.

The turning point was 1988. The Lakers and Dodgers both won championships that year. But while the Lakers went on to make six more appearances in the NBA finals and win three more championships, the Dodgers didn't win a single playoff series after that.

By the time the sports talk radio era came around in the 1990s, it was the Lakers who generated the most chatter. They had the better results and the bigger stars. Shaquille

O'Neal, Kobe Bryant, and all of their success and soap opera drama made the Lakers into not just the hottest story in town but one of the biggest stories in the country.

A survey taken by Loyola Marymount University in the mid-1990s showed that 77 percent of the fans had a favorable impression of the Lakers, and 71 percent of the Dodgers. And that was before the Lakers had their run of three consecutive championships to start the new century.

There's no need to take a poll now. Just look at the Lakers flags that fly from cars when the team does well. Check out all the Lakers jerseys around town.

Baseball was the national pastime. Following the Lakers is the local obsession.

WHICH LOCAL TEAM HAS THE BEST FANS?

5 Dodgers fans are more numerous. Lakers fans are more famous. But Kings fans are the most loyal.

No other fan base among the major pro sports has been asked to go so long with so little in return. Forty years of nothing.

As a post on the fan website Letsgokings.com noted: "Four times in franchise history the Kings have gone approximately 4 years or more between playoff game wins—1969–74, 1982–87, 1993–2001, and the current streak started in 2002. These droughts were marked by failing to reach the playoffs combined with being swept in whatever rounds they played in. The streak from 1993–2001 was nearly 8 years and game 1 of the 1993 Finals marked the Kings' final playoff victory of the 1990s. But we remain Kings fans anyway...."

Lakers fans are spoiled. God forbid the team go more than two years without making it to the NBA finals. The purple-and-gold crowd cries out, "This can't happen to us. Do something!"

Clippers fans have only recently found their own identity. When the team first moved here from San Diego in 1984, the early patrons were curious, or perhaps just fans of the NBA in general. They were grateful for the chance to buy tickets at cheaper prices than what the Lakers demanded, although Clippers games at the Sports Arena felt like Off Broadway theater compared to the grand events that were Lakers games at the Forum. Even when the two teams moved into the Staples Center, Clippers tickets for the exact same seat in the same building often cost half as much as a Lakers ticket. Now that the Clippers have been here for almost 25 years, there's a generation that's old enough to have come up preferring them, if that's their choice.

It's not easy to determine which is worse: following a team that's constantly downtrodden, or being teased with success the way Angels fans have been through the years. To be an Angels fan for the first four decades of their existence was to suffer through some of the most agonizing experiences in the history of baseball. But at least the team had a lovable owner in Gene Autry, the "Singing Cowboy," who often spent money on the team in a well intentioned but often misguided way. Sure, there was some frustration during the Disney years, but then the team won the World Series in 2002. And new owner Arturo Moreno came in and lowered the price of beer. Good times.

They have been coming out in red-clad droves ever since, even through the 77–85 "defense" of the championship in 2003. But it's hard to forget the numerous empty

21

sections of seats at Angel Stadium for a critical series against Oakland in September 2002, just a month before the World Series. It's a reminder that Angels games have only recently become a must-see event.

Dodgers fans have consistently come out to Chavez Ravine in large numbers. The problem is they aren't there very long. Most of the L.A. sports fans' reputation for coming late and leaving early is derived from those images of huge pockets of empty yellow seats in the stadium's prime areas during the first few innings of nationally televised games. And every time they replay that famous Kirk Gibson home run, there always will be that incriminating evidence of the car lights in the parking lot. The ultimate indictment of Dodgers fans: they left a close World Series game in the ninth inning.

Kings fans have never had the good or the bad exposed on such a national level. Except for the brief time after the Wayne Gretzky trade in 1988, Kings games have been the domain of a small, tight-knit fraternity. And ever since Phil Anschutz became the primary owner in 1995, the team has been stuck with leadership that always seemed to make half-hearted attempts to be competitive. They brought in sub-superstars, big names such as Ziggy Palffy, Jason Allison, and Adam Deadmarsh, who weren't quite franchise players. The moves were well-received, but after injuries wiped out Allison and Deadmarsh, the Kings got gun-shy.

Nevertheless, the Kings fans keep coming to Staples Center, keep following every little detail of the team, and keep rooting just as passionately. In a town where most of the intra-city pro sports rivalries are benevolent, Kings fans manage to work up a real hatred for that hockey team to the south, the Ducks.

That made it even twice as bad when the Ducks won the Stanley Cup in 2007. Their fans didn't have to suffer nearly long enough.

Dodgers fans didn't begrudge the Angels their World Series. When the Ducks won their championship, it tore up Kings fans. Just another sign that Kings fans are the best in town. At least that's one title they can celebrate.

SHOULD THOSE "BEAT L.A." CHANTS BE TAKEN AS A COMPLIMENT?

6 Let's put it this way: You never hear any crowds chanting, "Beat Cleveland."

Beating Los Angeles teams actually means something. There have been so many good teams in so many sports that defeating them can usually be considered a big accomplishment. Then there's the jealousy factor. Snowbound cities are envious of L.A.'s weather, and smaller Western cities are envious of L.A.'s size and economic might.

The question is, who has a right to say it? Technically, the "Beat L.A." chant belongs to Boston Celtics fans. Perhaps fans of the Philadelphia 76ers are entitled to say it as well, since it was Boston's request to them.

The chant originated in Boston Garden, near the end of Game 7 of the 1982 Eastern Conference finals. The series was the latest incarnation of a fierce rivalry that went back for two decades. Just the year before, the Celtics had come back from a 3–1 deficit in the series to beat Philadelphia. The situation nearly repeated itself in 1982, as the Celtics overcame another two-game deficit to force Game 7.

But this time, the 76ers refused to fold. They fought off

the Celtics, fought off the ghosts of Boston Garden, and fought off whatever doubts caused by the previous year had crept into their heads. In the final minutes, when the outcome was obvious, the Celtics fans stopped trying to root for a victory and accepted their fate. They just had one last request from their deathbed: "Beat L.A."

The chant grew louder and louder, until it turned into a demand. There was something admirable about it. It was an acknowledgment that, for all of their battles, they still had a greater common enemy. It was a statement that as much as we hate you, we hate them even more.

When the NBA finals began in Philadelphia, the fans greeted the Lakers with the new rallying cry. Undaunted, the Lakers won Game 1 and went on to win the series.

Over the years, the "Beat L.A." chant spread to other arenas around the NBA. It was heard in baseball stadiums when the Dodgers came to town—especially in San Francisco. It's usually accompanied by a pounding drumbeat to accent the chant's rhythmic cadence.

For the most part it's been an unmet request. The Lakers won, on average, one out of every three championships in the first 20 years after the chant began.

In the weird sense that "Remember the Alamo" is a tribute to what ultimately was defeat, the beginning of "Beat L.A." should be a reminder that those that try to usually don't.

7 Have you ever been at a large family gathering and realized you like your relatives better when they're not so close to you?

That's the principle that comes into play when L.A. teams try to bring local guys back home.

For whatever reason, it usually doesn't work out.

Maybe it's a need to put on a show. Maybe it's the constant ticket requests. Maybe it's the relatives who start coming out of the woodwork. But homecoming can be rough.

Los Angeles cultivated some of the best baseball talent in the country during the 1970s and early 1980s. But what happened when some of the game's brightest stars came back to wear Dodgers Blue? Disappointment.

Take Eric Davis. As a Cincinnati Red at age 27, he batted .281, hit 34 home runs, and drove in 101 runs in 127 games. After coming to his native Los Angeles as a Dodger at age 30, he hit .232 with 19 home runs and 85 RBI in 184 games. Back in Cincinnati at age 34, after a stop in Detroit, Davis hit .287 with 26 home runs and 83 RBI.

Darryl Strawberry went from hitting .265 with 37 home

runs and 108 RBI at age 28 in New York to hitting .265 with 28 home runs and 99 RBI at age 29 in Los Angeles. Then he got hurt, ran afoul of manager Tommy Lasorda, and played in only 75 games his final two years in Los Angeles.

Shawn Green's batting average plummeted 30 points—to .269—his first year after signing a free agent contract with the Dodgers. His home runs dropped from 42 to 24, and his RBI from 123 to 99.

Now some of the drop-off can be attributed to coming to Dodger Stadium, a pitcher-friendly park. And in Green's case, he made the move from the American to the National League.

But there's a prevailing theory that coming back home also subjects a player to all sorts of distractions: family and friends, community requests. Green was such a novelty as a Jewish star athlete that he was practically called upon to be a spokesman for the religion.

You can't blame ballpark configurations for statistical dips in basketball, where every court measures the same. But when Andre Miller, who is from Watts, came to the Clippers in a 2002 trade, he was a mere shadow of the player who had led the league in assists the previous season while in Cleveland. He seemed like the right piece: a heady point guard for a team that desperately needed one. But all of his shooting percentages declined, and he averaged only 6.7 assists per game with the Clippers, or four fewer than he did with the Cavaliers.

There were basketball issues, such as finding a place in the offense when Lamar Odom liked having the ball in his hands. There were also life-passage issues, such as when his stepfather died during the season.

And there were family issues, including a woman who kept calling the *Los Angeles Times* claiming she was a relative whom Miller was ignoring.

The late Dennis Johnson, who was born in San Pedro and was a Clippers assistant coach at the time, said, "For him, his family's all here, all his boys are here; that was one reason why I was glad I never got to come back to play. I never wanted to. You have all the pressures."

When Miller got to Denver for his next stop, his scoring average went up by more than a point and he had the three best shooting series of his career, much better than the career-low 40 percent he shot with the Clippers.

It doesn't seem to be as bad for people who grow up here and never leave, such as the Angels' Garret Anderson. He did just fine. If you never leave, people get used to you, the novelty of knowing someone on a local professional team wears off, and there are no instant demands for your time.

Los Angeles will always be a bountiful garden of athletic talent. So just a warning to the general managers: Draft the local boys. Just don't trade for them or sign them.

THE GOOD,
THE BAD, AND
THE UGLY

WHICH L.A. ATHLETE IS THE NO. 32?

8 Who's the first person you think of when you hear, "No. 32"? Your response could say a lot about you. It could give away your age, your background, and your preferences.

In the early 1960s, that number belonged to Sandy Koufax of the Dodgers. By the end of the decade, it was on the back of O. J. Simpson while he was scoring touchdowns at USC. In 1979 it was adopted by Magic Johnson (the No. 33 he wore at Michigan State was already taken on the Lakers by Kareem Abdul-Jabbar). And in the 1980s, Marcus Allen wore it on the Raiders.

All rank among the greatest at doing what they did. So who gets dibs on the jersey?

KOUFAX

The numbers: Career record of 165–87; 2.76 earned run average; 40 shutouts; 2,396 strikeouts; led the National League in strikeouts for five straight seasons; pitched four no-hitters, a record at the time.

The accolades: Hall of Fame, three-time Cy Young winner, plus National League MVP in 1963 and World Series MVP in 1963 and 1965.

SIMPSON

The numbers: Ran for 3,423 yards at USC; rushed for 1,880 yards his senior season, an NCAA record at the time; scored 26 touchdowns in 11 games; set or tied 19 NCAA, conference, and USC records.

The accolades: 1968 Heisman Trophy winner.

ALLEN

The numbers: Had 8,545 rushing yards (a Raiders record) and 4,258 receiving yards (fifth on the team's all-time list); scored 98 touchdowns; set an NFL single-season record in 1985 with 2,314 combined rushing and receiving yards and 14 touchdowns; set a Super Bowl record with a 74-yard touchdown run in Super Bowl XVIII.

The accolades: Hall of Fame, 1985 NFL MVP, Super Bowl XVIII MVP.

JOHNSON

The numbers: Had 10,141 assists (former record-holder, now third in NBA history); NBA-record 2,346 playoff assists; 138 "triple-doubles" (double figures in points, rebounds, and assists) in his career.

The accolades: NBA MVP three times (1987, 1989, 1990) and NBA finals MVP three times (1980, 1982, 1987); 11-time All-Star.

THE BREAKDOWN

Allen's case is diminished because he first burst onto the L.A. scene wearing No. 33 at USC. Plus, he finished his NFL career with the Kansas City Chiefs. And even though Allen had a longer and more productive career, the coolest Raiders jersey in the 1980s was Bo Jackson's No. 34.

Even though the "throwback" jersey fad began after the O. J. Simpson trial, you still saw people wearing the re-issues of his No. 32 Trojans jersey. Now there was an interesting fashion statement. It said: "I don't care what you think he did to his ex-wife and her friend, I'm wearing my O. J. jersey." Or it might have even been a deliberate attempt to provoke confrontation. Needless to say, anything that controversial would be a hard sell as the defining No. 32.

That leaves us with Koufax and Johnson. The problem that always comes back to hurt Koufax is the duration of his time at the top. Koufax's run of greatness lasted six years. Even though Johnson's career was abbreviated by his contraction of HIV, he still had the Lakers in the finals in his first year, in his 12th year, and seven other times in between. He was the dominant figure on the local sports scene throughout the 1980s, and when we think of a jersey with No. 32, we see Johnson's name above it.

WHO HAD THE BETTER ROOKIE SEASON, FERNANDO VALENZUELA OR MAGIC JOHNSON?

 9 They broke in a year apart. Magic Johnson was drafted by the Lakers in 1979, fresh off his NCAA championship with Michigan State. Then Fernando Valenzuela joined the Dodgers' big-league team on September 10, 1980, and he didn't allow an earned run in 10 relief appearances.

They both had their breakout moments when asked to be nothing more than a fill-in. During the fifth game of the 1980 NBA finals, Lakers center Kareem Abdul-Jabbar injured his ankle. He came back to finish the game and help the Lakers beat the Philadelphia 76ers, but afterward the swelling was so bad that he could not even make the trip to Philadelphia for Game 6.

No problem. The precocious Johnson, a 6-foot-9 guard, took Abdul-Jabbar's customary seat on the flight back east, then took Abdul-Jabbar's center position in the starting lineup. He delivered one of the greatest performances in NBA playoff history: 42 points, 15 rebounds, and 7 assists as the Lakers won the game and captured the first of their five championships of the 1980s.

The first start of the Dodgers' 1981 season was supposed to belong to Jerry Reuss. But Reuss pulled a hamstring muscle while shagging flies the day before. The Dodgers called on Valenzuela, who had pitched all of 18 innings in the major leagues. All Valenzuela did was throw a complete-game shutout at the Houston Astros. He won his first eight decisions, while allowing a miniscule .5 runs per nine innings over that span.

A strike interrupted the middle of the season, but Valenzuela and his dastardly screwball struck out a league-leading 180 batters in 25 starts and finished 13–7 with an earned run average of 2.48. He threw a complete game to win his lone World Series start.

Valenzuela and Johnson: two 20-year-olds who surpassed all expectations; two instant champions. But we'll look back on Valenzuela and see the greater historical impact. It wasn't just that Valenzuela became the first Rookie of the Year to also win the Cy Young award, while Johnson didn't even win the NBA's Rookie of the Year award (an honor that went to Boston's Larry Bird).

Valenzuela was more than a phenom, he was a phenomenon. Johnson represented a changing style, a man who could adapt to any position on the court and implored everyone wearing the same color jersey to keep up with his fast pace. And while Valenzuela brought his own distinctive flavor to the pitcher's mound, with the high leg kick and the last-second glance to the heavens before he delivered the ball, Valenzuela was also a movement. "Fernandomania," they called it. Dodger Stadium crowds would swell when he pitched, sometimes topping 50,000. A couple of radio talk show hosts even tried to rename the San Fernando Valley as the San Fernando Valenzuela.

Valenzuela energized the city's sizable Mexican-American community, giving them a mainstream idol. Some even credit him for starting the influx of Latino players who impacted every aspect of the game over the next 20 years.

WHAT WAS THE WORST TRADE IN LOS ANGELES HISTORY?

As bad as trading Shaquille O'Neal for Lamar Odom, Brian Grant, and Caron Butler was at the time, it wasn't the worst transaction in the history of Los Angeles sports.

At least the Lakers could say they had O'Neal at his best, and they reaped the benefits: three championships for the team and one MVP season for Shaq. If you sell your house before the market peaks, at least you still profited from the appreciation—and in the meantime you had a place to live.

The worst trades are the equivalent of selling at the bottom, then watching the market take off.

That's why the Rams' trade of Eric Dickerson, while delivering a mortal wound to the team's chances of staying in Anaheim, doesn't go down as the city's worst. Dickerson had his three best rushing seasons and his only two playoff victories with the Rams.

Even the Kings got away with trading Wayne Gretzky to St. Louis for Patrice Tardif, Roman Vopat, and Craig Johnson without it coming back to haunt them. The Great One's presence couldn't help the Kings qualify for the playoffs the previous two seasons, and they were on their way to another early vacation when Gretzky requested the trade. He was on the decline. He never again matched the 38 goals he scored in his last season as a King, and neither the Blues nor his final team, the New York Rangers, reached the Stanley Cup finals with him on the roster.

The truly agonizing, one-that-got-away trade in Los Angeles history was when the Dodgers traded Pedro Martinez to the Montreal Expos for Delino DeShields.

And to think, the origin of this misguided trade came when second baseman Jody Reed misjudged the market after one year with the Dodgers. As then-Dodgers general manager Fred Claire recounted in his book *My 30 Years in Dodger Blue*, he offered Reed a three-year, $7.8 million deal with a base salary starting at $2 million in 1994. Reed, coming off a season in which he hit .276, thought he could do better. His agent wanted $11.25 million over three years. Reed wound up signing with the Milwaukee Brewers and making $750,000 in 1994.

When it became evident that Reed was going elsewhere, Claire decided to go shopping for another second baseman. Martinez was coming off his first full season, when he went 10–5 with a 3.93 earned run average. What caught the Expos' eye were Martinez's 119 strikeouts (against only 57 walks) in 107 innings. You bet they made that deal.

Martinez won a Cy Young award in Montreal. If it's any consolation to the Dodgers, the Expos didn't get his full services, either. Rather than lose him to free agency they traded him to Boston in 1997. With the Red Sox he won two more Cy Young awards—and threw seven shutout innings in Game 3 of the 2004 World Series during his final start for them.

All told, 196 of his 206 victories through 2006 came after he left the Dodgers. So did 2,871 of his 2,998 strikeouts.

DeShields hit .241 in three seasons with the Dodgers. In the playoffs in 1995 and 1996 he was 3 for 16.

To quote Claire: "The trade just didn't work out for the Dodgers."

Which is a little like saying *Howard the Duck* didn't work out for Universal Pictures.

History isn't kind when you trade away someone on the brink of a Hall of Fame career, and get so little in return.

WHICH L.A. ATHLETE WAS THE GREATEST FREE AGENT SIGNING IN HISTORY?

Ideally, there are three things you want to get from a free agent signing: a championship, an MVP award, and a box office boost.

Shaquille O'Neal hit the trifecta unlike any other signing in pro sports. The Lakers won three championships with O'Neal. He won the NBA finals MVP for each, in addition to the regular season MVP in 2000. And a team that drew 15,845 fans per game to the Forum the season before he arrived drew 17,003 in his first season, then regularly played to sold-out houses once the Lakers moved to Staples Center.

Come playoff time, the building is more like "$taples Center."

Playoff games are when teams really do damage at the cash register. Not only are the ticket prices higher, but the player salaries have already been paid out. Winning time is also cha-ching time. The Lakers, who had won only one playoff series since Magic Johnson retired in 1991, played 61 home playoff games while O'Neal was in town.

You won't find another free agent who can match that success across the board

Free agency has only been around since 1975. Five years after an unsuccessful court challenge to baseball's reserve system by Curt Flood, an independent arbitrator ruled that baseball players Andy Messersmith and Peter McNally did not have to accept contract renewals with their old teams.

The Yankees (not surprisingly) were among the first to take advantage of the new sports landscape. They scooped up Reggie Jackson and Catfish Hunter, who played on New York's back-to-back World Series championship teams in 1977 and 1978, with Jackson winning the 1977 World Series MVP.

Barry Bonds won five MVP awards after he signed with San Francisco in 1993, but never won the championship. Greg Maddux won a lone championship in Atlanta to go with his three Cy Young awards after he left the Chicago Cubs.

The most significant player moves in hockey—Wayne Gretzky to the Kings in 1988 and Mark Messier to the New York Rangers in 1991—were both trades.

Free agency came a little bit later to football, and the most significant free agent was Reggie White. The defensive lineman was part Curt Flood, part Shaq. He was a plaintiff in the lawsuit that brought about free agency to the NFL, then he signed with the Green Bay Packers in

1993. He said his choice was directed by God. In Wisconsin, they'd tell you God is a Packers fan.

White's signing encouraged other players to come to Green Bay, which isn't the most glamorous spot in the NFL world. And he anchored the defensive line that won the Super Bowl in 1997.

Still, none of those names could match O'Neal's trophy collection. In retrospect, maybe Jerry West wasn't exaggerating when he likened the Lakers' signing of O'Neal to the birth of his own children.

Even though many viewed it as a fait accompli before the free agency process started, O'Neal's signing with the Lakers wasn't always a slam dunk.

He and his family had a home base in Orlando (he still has a house there a decade after he left the Magic).

But he did start to feel uncomfortable when the locals criticized O'Neal for having a child out of wedlock.

And when negotiations started, the Magic didn't blow him away. They started off with a four-year, $55 million offer. Even the Washington Bullets (as they were then known, when they also were known for being cheap) made a bigger initial offer than that to Juwan Howard.

Very early in the free agent market, Alonzo Mourning established the true starting price for O'Neal. Throughout the season, in the buildup to free agency, O'Neal had used a luxury car comparison when discussing the price difference between Mourning and O'Neal.

"If you pay $30,000 for a Beemer, you've got to pay $50,000 for a Benz," O'Neal said.

And which type of car would that make O'Neal? "I'm a Benz, bro."

In order to go shopping at the Mercedes-Benz dealership, the Lakers had to shed contracts to make enough room under the salary cap.

The Lakers traded Vlade Divac ($4.5 million) to Charlotte for the rights to draft pick Kobe Bryant. Most people simply saw it as a salary dump, not realizing that the Lakers had just secured the second part of the 1–2 punch that dominated the early 2000 years.

The Lakers came at O'Neal with an offer for $98 million over seven years. That wasn't even as much as the BMW.

Orlando came back with a $115 million offer. The Lakers cleared more salary cap space by trading George Lynch and Anthony Peeler, and finally put forth a $120 million offer.

Orlando was done with the bidding. And O'Neal was done with Orlando after residents voted overwhelmingly against O'Neal when the local newspaper asked if he was worth $115 million a year. The Magic took the same stance. Even though NBA rules gave them the ability to top the Lakers' offer, Orlando never bothered.

And O'Neal turned into the best $120 million investment in sports history.

WHAT IS THE GREATEST INDIVIDUAL STREAK BY AN L.A. ATHLETE?

12 Streaks are the most impressive records because there's a sense of urgency inherent in every competition. They aren't a drawn-out march to a sometimes inevitable conclusion, like a career record. They must be renewed every day. The longer they go on, the clearer it becomes that this is a chance that won't repeat itself. The drama sucks in even the casual fan.

We won't count the streaks of individual athletes who were from the Los Angeles area. So there will be no trophy for Tiger Woods, from Cypress, for winning four consecutive majors. No award for Pete Sampras, who grew up in Palos Verdes, for finishing as the No. 1-ranked player on the ATP tour for six consecutive years. They didn't do it in Los Angeles or for Los Angeles. So that leaves us with:

3. KOBE BRYANT'S FOUR CONSECUTIVE GAMES OF SCORING 50 OR MORE POINTS

Maybe this doesn't get full appreciation, because Bryant makes it look so easy. You get the sense he could score 50 points whenever he wants to, and certainly any time he has been given the go-ahead to shoot as much as he wants. With Phil Jackson authorizing this mission because the rest of the team was struggling to score points, Bryant launched 140 shots over a four-game stretch.

It started when he went for 65 points against the Portland Trail Blazers in an overtime game on March 16, 2007. Even though he played 50 minutes that night, when the Lakers played Minnesota two days later, Bryant scored 50 more. He scored 60 points against Memphis on March 22, and the very next night he played all but one minute against the New Orleans Hornets and produced another 50-point night. That moved Bryant past Elgin Baylor and Michael Jordan, leaving him alone in the room with Wilt Chamberlain as the only players to do it four times in a row.

Ah, Chamberlain: the guy who always seems to put scoring accomplishments in perspective. As the prolific scorer George Gervin once said, "He IS the record book. You think you've broken some records? Go deeper in the book. He'll humble you."

And that's where Bryant's serial scoring binge comes up short. Wilt did it five consecutive times. And six. And seven. Three separate streaks that topped Bryant's in NBA history.

If you want a record, try...

2. ERIC GAGNE'S 84 CONSECUTIVE SAVES

Gagne beat Tom Gordon's old consecutive saves mark by 30—a Bob Beamon-like jump into the record books. And while Gagne was getting the job done 84 straight times, other relievers around baseball blew a combined 969 saves.

Just as remarkable might have been Gagne's impact on Dodgers fans. He actually made it cool to stay until the ninth inning. When Gagne was at his peak in 2003 and 2004, his entrance into the game was the most exciting moment in L.A. sports. "Welcome to the Jungle" blasted from the speakers, "Game Over" flashed on the scoreboard, and the town went crazy. With Shaquille O'Neal traded and Bryant trying to resuscitate his image after being accused of sexual assault, Gagne reigned as the city's favorite athlete.

For a stretch that lasted almost two years, every time Gagne came out of the bullpen in a save situation, it meant not only his streak was on the line...the game was on the line as well. Talk about pressure. Failure wouldn't just end his streak, it could cost his team a victory.

But there is a little bit of leeway in the job of a closer. He can enter the game with a three-run lead, give up two runs, and still get credit for the save. If the base runners were inherited, they won't even count against his earned run average. That's why, taking into account the zero tolerance for error required to sustain it, the most impressive individual streak is:

1. OREL HERSHISER'S 59 CONSECUTIVE SHUTOUT INNINGS

Hershiser's performance wasn't just remarkable, it was clutch.

The Dodgers were in the thick of a pennant race when it started with four scoreless innings in Montreal on August 30. Then he pitched shutouts in his next five starts. Five straight shutouts! The major league baseball leaders in 2006 had three shutouts for the entire season.

By the time he made his final start of the season, the Dodgers had clinched the division. All eyes were on Hershiser. But even another shutout would leave him $\frac{2}{3}$ of an inning short of Don Drysdale's record 58 $\frac{2}{3}$ shutout innings. Hershiser threw another scoreless nine innings, then got a bonus: the Dodgers were scoreless as well, forcing extra innings. Hershiser pitched the 10th and got the record (although the Dodgers wound up losing in 16 innings).

Most of the starts were as pressure-packed as a Gagne close-out. But while Gagne's earned run average of 0.82 during his streak was microscopic, nothing beats nothing. In the month of September, Hershiser didn't give up a run: 55 innings and a spotless 0.00 ERA. Five shutouts in one month. Keep in mind that the most Randy Johnson ever had in one season was six. Greg Maddux's best was only five. (Hershiser had eight for that entire season.)

Hershiser had no room for a mistake. Even Gagne allowed three home runs during his save streak. No one could say they took Hershiser deep during his streak. They couldn't even say they reached home plate.

Gagne usually could get the job done with only three outs. By the time batters figured out what he was throwing, the game was over.

Hershiser had to go through the lineup three and four times, and still they couldn't figure him out.

Almost 20 years later, we've got it all processed. It's the best run an L.A. athlete ever had.

WHAT WAS THE GREATEST LOS ANGELES TEAM STREAK?

In other cities, streaks can be signs of futility. Take Chicago, where the Cubs are working on 100 years without a World Series championship and the Northwestern football team once lost a record-setting 34 consecutive games.

Los Angeles squads set successful streak standards (how's that for alliteration—a streak of five consecutive S's). The challenge is ranking them. Here's one try.

4. THE DODGERS START THE SAME FOUR INFIELDERS FOR 8 ½ CONSECUTIVE YEARS

First baseman Steve Garvey, second baseman Davey Lopes, third baseman Ron Cey, and shortstop Bill Russell first saw their names at those positions together on the lineup card on June 13, 1973. Over the next nine years they became the definition of fixtures, the same guys at the same positions all the way through the 1981 season.

The dates are significant because they span the advent of free agency. And yet the team still held together. Garvey epitomized the group's stability, playing in 1,207 consecutive games. Then again, Garvey also started the breakup, leaving as a free agent in 1982.

Obviously they had to be doing something right to stick together that long, and their run did encompass four trips to the World Series and one championship. But this streak was more a testament to stability than success, which is why it gets the lowest ranking.

Just to show how remarkable the feat was, the Angels, by comparison, had seven different infield combinations in their Opening Day starting lineups during that same span.

3. UCLA'S BASKETBALL TEAM WINS 88 CONSECUTIVE GAMES

Let's give this the proper perspective. Even if you take away the last 15 games of the 1970–71 season (which the Bruins all won), and even if you take away the first 13 games of the 1973–74 season (which the Bruins all won), that leaves back-to-back undefeated seasons in 1971–72 and 1972–73. Two undefeated seasons. Since that year there has been only one undefeated college basketball team: the 1975–76 Indiana Hoosiers.

Now add the 28 other games the Bruins won to begin and end the streak, and that's practically another season's worth. Three undefeated seasons from one school over three years, while every other Division I college basketball program in the country has produced exactly one in almost 35 years.

49

2. THE 1971–72 LAKERS WIN 33 CONSECUTIVE GAMES

Not only the top mark in the NBA, but in all of professional sports. The other top streaks: 26 consecutive victories by the New York Giants in Major League Baseball, 21 by the New England Patriots in the NFL, and 17 by the Pittsburgh Penguins in the National Hockey League.

What makes the Lakers' streak more impressive is that NBA teams have the most difficult travel schedules of any sport. This was especially true in 1971–72, before the days of charter flights or private planes for NBA teams. They all flew commercial back then, which often meant early wake-up calls for the first flight out of town the morning after playing, and arriving in a new town the day of a game. And back then, teams played on three consecutive nights, a scheduling cruelty that was subsequently dropped by the NBA. The Lakers had four sets of back-to-back-to-backs during their 33-game streak, which makes it even more impressive that there wasn't a letdown.

But this was still one team playing exceptionally well for a stretch. For duration of peak performance, it can't match…

1. UCLA WINS 7 CONSECUTIVE NCAA CHAMPIONSHIPS

One other way to look at this, if you break it down: In the course of this streak, UCLA accounted for three of the eight back-to-back championship teams in basketball history.

One other thing to keep in mind: At the time, freshmen were not eligible to play for varsity basketball, so seven years represented more than two complete cycles of players. This wasn't the same team establishing itself and settling into a groove. No singular player provided the backbone of the dynasty, as Bill Russell did for the Boston Celtics.

It comes back to John Wooden, his coaching, his system, and his program. From Lew Alcindor, Lynn Shackelford, Lucious Allen, and Mike Warren to Sidney Wicks, Henry Bibby, and John Vallely, to Bill Walton, Larry Farmer, and Keith Wilkes: different players, same results.

Some people dock the Bruins because the smaller size of the NCAA tournament field required only four victories to win it all. But even with the 65-team tournament today, the seeding process practically guarantees an opening-round victory for top seeds. It might as well be a bye.

And besides, maybe we shouldn't think of them as seven four-game winning streaks. How about one 28-game winning streak in tournament games? Several teams combining to take out the top-level competition again and again, resulting in a streak that almost equaled the Lakers' streak. That's why this streak surpasses it.

WHAT'S THE BETTER RIVALRY: DODGERS–GIANTS OR LAKERS–CELTICS?

It's not easy for a Los Angeles resident to work up a good hatred for some other place.

Sure, the ugly adjectives are constantly hurled toward the Southland: fake, smoggy, traffic-congested, sprawling. And then there's the criticism about the lack of seasonal change—as if East Coast residents are celebrating while shoveling off the driveway on the third consecutive sub-freezing day.

For the most part, the citizens of L.A. respond to all the negative comments with a big collective, "Whatever." Then they hop out of their pool, hop into their cars, and open up the sunroof. Life's too good to worry about what they're thinking about elsewhere.

But certain sights can bring out the Angeleno's hidden temper. Among those are the green and white of the Boston Celtics or the orange and black of the San Francisco Giants.

The Lakers–Celtics beef started in the 1960s, when the two teams met in the NBA finals six times. The Celtics won all of them, so in that sense it could not truly be called a rivalry—one side never had something the other desired. Still, the futility just made the Lakers and their fans hate the Celtics that much more. They hated Bill Russell's cackle. They hated the smug look on Red Auerbach's face when he lit up a victory cigar.

It was renewed in the 1980s, and this time on more even terms. After the Celtics beat the Lakers in a bitter seven-game series in 1984 (giving Larry Bird a bit of revenge in his personal rivalry with Magic Johnson that went back to the 1979 NCAA championship), the Lakers beat them in 1985 and 1987.

In the process, a whole new generation of Lakers fans learned to hate the Celtics. There were new foils, such as Danny Ainge's Dennis-the-Mennis face, Kevin McHale's physique that was reminiscent of Lurch from *The Addams Family*, or even Dennis Johnson's freckles. And Auerbach was still around in a front office role from the Celtics.

And there were new battle lines being drawn. There was the time McHale clotheslined Kurt Rambis. Or the time James Worthy and Greg Kite were scrapping on the floor. Or the time Magic and Bob McAdoo were shoving McHale back and forth like a pinball.

Because the schedule only called for them to play twice in the regular season, the majority of their meetings from 1984–87 came in the NBA finals, when everything was at stake and the passion flowed over.

Then the Celtics dropped off. Their most recent NBA finals appearance was 1987, while the Lakers made it back seven times since then. These days, Lakers–Celtics feels more like just another game.

By contrast, the Giants and Dodgers never met in the postseason, not even in the wild card era. It's a rivalry based more on proximity than anything else. It started back in New York and continued after the Giants followed the Dodgers to California. Instead of intra-city supremacy, they now represented two distinctly different populaces.

But something evolved that made this the city's best rivalry. Unlike the Lakers and the Celtics, who had a championship at stake for both teams, Dodgers–Giants can matter even if it's the first week of the season, or even if one team is hopelessly out of it.

And that's the greatest part. When keeping the other guys from being happy means just as much as making yourself happy, that's a rivalry.

The infamous "Joe Morgan Game" is the ultimate example. In 1982, the Dodgers won the first two games against the Giants in the final weekend of the season. In the process, they eliminated the Giants. The Dodgers still needed to win on Sunday to get in the playoffs. Then Morgan crushed their hopes with a three-run home run in the seventh inning, in a game the Giants won 5–3.

Years later, former Giant Duane Kuiper told the *San Francisco Chronicle*: "I still remember watching Joe between first and second base. He raised his right arm as if to say, 'If we're not going to win it, you're not either.'"

Morgan explained the uncharacteristic emotional outburst by saying, "I have a lot of respect and admiration for the Dodgers. But I wanted this one for the Giants and the fans."

Rivalries are more about the fans than the players, especially in the era of free agency. Players used to play for rivals. They used to play with players on their rivals. And every team is a potential employer.

But for the fans, rivalries enhance the whole sporting experience.

Sports are supposed to provide an outlet from real tensions, to give superiority via surrogates.

Twenty-two years after the Joe Morgan home run, the Dodgers had their revenge. In 2004 it was Dodgers fans who rejoiced on the season's final day. The Dodgers trailed 3–0 in the bottom of the ninth, but rallied for seven runs. The last four came on a Steve Finley grand slam that sent the Dodgers to the playoffs.

Just as importantly, it sent the Giants home.

WHAT WAS THE BEST L.A. SPORTS YEAR?

15 For a city that's had multiple teams succeed in every sport, the best year would have to be one with multiple championships.

For football seasons we'll count the calendar year, not the season year. College football and the NFL play their big bowl games in January (or February for the Super Bowl), so, for example, USC's 1972 national championship team was actually crowned in 1973.

That technicality prevented 1972 from being the only triple-championship year from our tally, which starts in the 1960s to account for the arrival of the Lakers and the rise to power of UCLA's basketball program. In 1972 the Lakers won their 69th game to set an NBA standard for excellence and captured their first championship in Los Angeles, Bill Walton won his first championship with the UCLA basketball team, and Coach John McKay's Trojans football went undefeated in the regular season, on its way to becoming the first unanimous No. 1 team in both the coaches and media polls.

In addition to the revenue sports at the two big schools, the other teams surveyed were the Lakers, Dodgers, Angels, Clippers, Kings, and Ducks.

We can't account for every championship in every sport,

so apologies to the likes of the 2002 MLS Cup-winning Galaxy or the 2002 WNBA champion Sparks. Actually, including them would have made 2002 a runaway winner, with the Lakers' three-peat and the Angels' breakthrough World Series championship joining the Galaxy and Sparks in the winners circle.

But how many commemorative Galaxy championship caps and T-shirts did you see around town that year?

We're going with a year that would have caused the greatest "We're Number One" feeling of civic pride among the most people possible.

That would be 1988 A.D.

In June the Lakers won their second consecutive championship, just barely making good on Pat Riley's repeat guarantee by winning three Game 7s. It certified the 1980s as the Lakers' decade in the NBA.

In October, the Dodgers won the World Series in as memorable a five-game set as you'll ever see, starting with Kirk Gibson's dramatic home run in Game 1 and ending with Orel Hershiser on the mound in Game 5. It capped off a record-setting season for Hershiser, who would be named *Sports Illustrated's* Sportsman of the Year.

And in between the Lakers and Dodgers triumphs, the Kings traded for Wayne Gretzky.

So in 1988, not only was Los Angeles the home of the best teams in basketball and baseball, it also became the epicenter of hockey.

57

Gretzky's arrival completed the stable of superstars in Los Angeles. The greatest hockey player skated at the Forum, where he would soon become its all-time leading goal scorer. The NBA's all-time leading scorer, Kareem Abdul-Jabbar, already played there. So did Magic Johnson (even if 1988 was the one year in a four-year span he did not win the MVP award). The Dodgers had that year's MVP in Gibson and Cy Young award winner in Hershiser.

The Raiders' backfield featured Bo Jackson and Marcus Allen. Jim Everett threw a league-leading 31 touchdowns for the Rams that season.

It was the Los Angeles we all imagine, abundant to the point of excess, a showcase of talent, a collection of winners. It was the best year ever to be a sports fan in the city.

WHAT WAS THE WORST CALL THAT WENT AGAINST A LOCAL TEAM?

16 The 2005 Angels could overcome unfair scheduling, an overnight flight, and jet lag. Asking them to overcome a free base-runner and an extra out given to the Chicago White Sox on the infamous A.J. Pierzynski play was just too much.

After beating the Yankees in Game 5 of the Division Series in Anaheim on October 10, the Angels flew to Chicago for Game 1 of the American League championship series the next day. Unfair? Certainly. But baseball was beholden to the television schedule, and it dictated the league championship series had to start then, on that day.

The Angels didn't get to their Chicago hotel until 6:30 a.m. But thanks to a home run by Garret Anderson and a good start by Paul Byrd, the Angels grabbed an early 3–0 lead and hung on to win 3–2.

Game 2 entered the late innings tied at 1–1. The Angels brought Kelvin Escobar in to pitch in the seventh inning and were confident the converted starter could last a while—potentially long enough to give a lead to closer Francisco Rodriguez.

He looked like he had escaped the bottom of the ninth

inning when, with two outs, he got Pierzynski to swing and miss at strike three. Angels catcher Josh Paul nabbed the ball with his mitt just above the dirt. Home plate umpire Doug Eddings made a "punch out" motion, which everyone interpreted as an out call.

Later, Eddings would introduce the defining word of the series when he said the apparent out motion was merely his "mechanic" for calling a strike.

Paul rolled the ball back toward the mound and started to leave. Pierzynski was about to head back to the dugout, then realized he had not been called out, and hustled toward first base. It was as if Pierzynski sold Eddings on the call and Eddings chose to believe that the ball bounced before Paul caught it, meaning that Paul had to tag Pierzynski to record the out.

Pierzynski was ruled safe at first. Pablo Ozuna pinch-ran for him, stole second base, and scored the game-winning run on a base hit by Joe Crede.

At a news conference afterward, Eddings and umpire supervisor Rick Reiker insisted that Eddings had not made an out call and that the replay did not indicate Paul caught the ball—even though most other observers thought he did.

"At this point, I would say at best it's inconclusive," Reiker said.

We're left to draw our own conclusions then, and we can deduce that the Angels never recovered from that stunning turn in the series. The Angels had a chance to come back to Anaheim with a 2–0 lead and momentum. They should have been satisfied with getting a split in Chicago, but they couldn't seem to get the bad call out of their heads. Their fans sure couldn't, booing Eddings whenever he made a call at Angel Stadium...or even when balls were hit near his position along the outfield line.

The Angels did not win another game. Amazingly, White Sox manager Ozzie Guillen didn't use his bullpen for the rest of the series, as Mark Buerhle, Jon Garland, Freddy Garcia, and Jose Contreras logged complete games. The White Sox certainly outplayed the Angels the rest of the way. But one wonders if they could have won four straight games without the help of that gift run in the ninth inning of Game 2. Sometimes all it takes is one victory to change a series around, as that one demonstrated.

It had to be particularly devastating to the Angels as they watched the White Sox roll over the Houston Astros in the World Series. If the National League was going to put up so little resistance, it meant another championship was there for the taking.

Instead, they got the treatment familiar to so many people driving lemon cars: they were robbed by a mechanic.

WHAT WAS THE BIGGEST BREAK AN L.A. TEAM GOT FROM THE OFFICIALS?

If you asked this question in Sacramento you'd get a unanimous answer. It would have to be the break that the 2002 Lakers got in the Western Conference finals against the Sacramento Kings.

Without the officials erroneously counting a Samaki Walker three-point heave that came after the halftime buzzer—a play that would have been reviewable by instant replay under rules implemented the following season—that Robert Horry shot at the end of Game 4 wouldn't have meant a thing. And don't get the Northern Californians started on the officiating in Game 6, when the Lakers shot a staggering 27 free throws in the fourth quarter. That one so incensed consumer advocate Ralph Nader that he fired off a letter to NBA commissioner David Stern.

Sorry, but Sacramento fans should save their protests for the government, and Nader can go back to demanding car recalls. The officials didn't give the Lakers that series.

People conveniently forget the ball that should have been

called out of bounds on Chris Webber in Game 6. Instead, possession was awarded to the Kings, and Mike Bibby made a go-ahead shot. People also forget that somehow Bobby Jackson untucked Kobe Bryant's jersey and wasn't called for a foul when Bryant missed an attempted game-winning shot at the buzzer. And even after the Game 6 debacle, the Kings still had the chance they played all season for, a Game 7 at home, and they blew it by making only 16 out of 30 free throws and losing in overtime. Oh, and Kings guard Doug Christie later admitted he was "scared to death" in that game. Does that sound like a team that was unjustly denied a conference championship?

No, the team with the legitimate gripe when it comes to L.A. breaks resides in Ann Arbor, Michigan. Football teams don't have an entire series to let the breaks even out. They only get one game. And in the 1979 Rose Bowl, the Michigan Wolverines got robbed.

In the second quarter, USC running back Charles White took off for the end zone from Michigan's 3-yard line. He lost the ball, and Michigan linebacker Jerry Meter recovered the fumble at the 1-yard line. But Gil Marchman, the head linesman, ruled that White had crossed the goal line and awarded USC a touchdown. That gave the Trojans a 14–3 lead, in a game they wound up winning 17–10.

Even the USC media guide's recap of the game acknowledges that White's touchdown was "disputed." But it doesn't take away from its share of the national championship

63

awarded by the UPI coaches poll that season, one of the 11 national championships the university counts.

It also meant the Pacific-10 won its fifth consecutive game against the Big Ten in the Rose Bowl, and Michigan Coach Bo Schembechler remained winless in the Pasadena New Year's Day game. He would have to wait another two years for his first Rose Bowl victory.

WHAT WAS THE GREATEST GOOSE-BUMP MOMENT IN A LOS ANGELES STADIUM?

Some of the greatest sports moments didn't involve a ball or a puck. They were the times the games receded to the backdrop, and the drama of the human experience took over. We paused to celebrate life, to recognize not just the athletic accomplishments, but also the people behind them.

In sheer volume, nothing could top Roy Campanella Night at the Coliseum on May 7, 1959. The largest crowd in baseball history came out to honor a man who never played a game in Los Angeles.

That showed the respect people had for Campanella, the great Dodgers catcher in their Brooklyn days who was one of the first to follow Jackie Robinson across baseball's color line. Campanella was driving home on Long Island on January 28, 1958, when he lost control of his car and hit a telephone pole. He was paralyzed from the shoulder down and spent the rest of his life in a wheelchair.

That year, the Dodgers played their first season in Los

Angeles. Campanella would say one of the biggest regrets of his life was that he didn't get to play there with them.

At the time, he had greater concerns. He had to sell his house to pay his mounting medical bills. His wife left him.

But through his adversity, he found out just how much people cared for him. The Dodgers arranged for an in-season exhibition game to raise funds for him. No less an attraction than the New York Yankees—the No. 1 draw in sports—came all the way across the country to provide the opposition. More than 93,000 people packed the Coliseum and an additional 15,000 were turned away. Campanella received $75,000 from the proceeds.

The highlight of the night came when former Dodgers teammate Pee Wee Reese wheeled Campanella out on the field as the lights dimmed and the fans lit matches, making the Coliseum look like a field filled with fireflies on a summer evening. And that's when it kicked in, the moment that produced the unforgettable image of Campanella being silently serenaded by thousands of lights.

Campanella was in tears when he said, "This is something I will never forget. I thank God I'm here living to be able to see it. It's a wonderful thing."

The second-most chilling moment occurred in the same venue, during the opening ceremonies of the 1984 Olympics. This moment had elements of suspense as well, as the world waited to find out who would have the honor of lighting the Olympic flame to commence the Games.

They were the final steps of the Olympic torch's 82-day, 9,320-mile trek across America, and the organizers did a masterful job of keeping the identity of the final carrier a secret. Gina Hemphill, granddaughter of Jesse Owens, turned out to be the next-to-last. She handed off to Rafer Johnson, the Gold Medal winner in the decathlon at the 1960 Olympics in Rome.

He headed toward the steps at the peristyle end of the Coliseum, and as he ascended, another set of steps was rising to bring him up near the top of the arches, giving him 92 steps to negotiate in all.

When he reached the top of the ramp, he held the torch high, showing it to the fans in the stands and the millions watching on television. They didn't know that he had battled shin splints and wasn't sure he could run all the way to the top. His triumph—making it up all those steps at age 49—was our triumph. We all gazed at him while we wondered what the view was like from his perch, from a newly created vantage point high above the Coliseum field, where athletes from around the world had gathered.

Johnson invited everyone to share in the moment. As he held the flame to a fuse, the fire spread to a set of Olympic rings, then to the cauldron at the top of the Coliseum.

It was happening. An Olympics that no one wanted, that so many doubted could be pulled off successfully, was officially open for business.

Let the goose bumps begin.

WHAT WAS THE BEST GROUP NICKNAME FOR A LOS ANGELES TEAM?

No need to debate the best individual nickname. Magic, hands down. It didn't take long after Earvin Johnson got to town for the quotation marks and/or parentheses to be dropped. You really didn't need the last name, either. All you had to say was Magic and everyone knew the subject. The nickname—bestowed upon him by a sportswriter in his hometown of East Lansing, Michigan—was the perfect description for his game, and a dream for headline writers. Case closed.

Group nicknames—now that's a different matter. Los Angeles has been blessed with several teams that held distinctive monikers, including "The Lake Show" and "The Wild Bunch."

The "Showtime" Lakers of the 1980s were awe-inspiring in their own right. They won with flash and flair, with Magic Johnson leading a style of play that was as entertaining as it was effective. The Lakers played high-speed basketball that would fast-break opponents into submission, a method that led to five championships throughout the decade and thrilled fans along the way.

To this day, "Showtime" conjures up images of Magic Johnson grinning, or throwing a no-look pass to James Worthy, or Pat Riley roaming the sidelines in his Armani suit. Or even Dancing Barry strutting around during timeouts.

The only problem with "Showtime" is that the word doesn't stand on its own. You always hear it paired with another word. They were the "Showtime" Lakers, or it was the "Showtime" Era. But at least that team had a description that fit them. The championship teams of the early 2000s, led by Shaquille O'Neal and Kobe Bryant, never had a catchy nickname. Even the group that preceded them, led by Nick Van Exel, Eddie Jones, and Elden Campbell, had "The Lake Show." A nice little nickname, but it didn't define a winning period.

A nickname that once worked, but subsequently was worn into the ground, was the "Gutty Little Bruins" UCLA football team of 1965. The undersized squad, featuring Bob Stiles, Jim Colletto, Russ Banduci, and future UCLA coach Terry Donahue, beat top-ranked Michigan State in the Rose Bowl that season. But people couldn't just let that nickname be. Any time a future UCLA team overachieved, someone would feel compelled to label them gutty or little or both. Nicknames should be defining...not clichéd.

The best of all of them was "The Fearsome Foursome," the description applied to the Rams' defensive line in the 1960s. You don't want sports nicknames to be too cute, and this one was in no danger of making people say, "Aww, how nice."

How many nicknames give you alliteration, rhyme, and such a perfect meter, to borrow a few poetry terms?

It was so good that they even rotated individual members in, but still kept the name—kind of like the Temptations. The original group consisted of Deacon Jones, Lamar Lundy, Merlin Olsen, and Rosey Grier. Roger Brown replaced Grier in 1967, and the hits just kept on coming. In fact, you could argue they hit their peak the next year, when they set a record for fewest yards allowed in a 14-game season.

But they were always just as fierce as their nickname, led by the head-slapping Jones, who is credited with creating the term *quarterback sack*. Why that term? "You know, you sack a city, you devastate it," Jones once said. The "Fearsome Foursome" pillaged their way through the NFL—with a nickname alone that could make opponents tremble.

Believe it or not, the best comeback did not occur in the game known as "The Comeback."

The Trojans wiped out a big deficit in that 1974 USC–Notre Dame game, but in retrospect they had more than a half of a football game to score three touchdowns (plus two-point conversions). It was only an 18-point deficit after Anthony Davis caught a touchdown pass with 10 seconds left in the first half, and just a 12-point margin when Davis returned the opening kick of the second half for a 102-yard touchdown. USC had plenty of time remaining and took full advantage of it, prevailing 55–24.

The best comeback has to be more than a comeback. It has to be miraculous.

That's where the Kings come in to swoop the greatest comeback award, for "The Miracle on Manchester" against the Edmonton Oilers in 1982. It contains all of the three C's, to their fullest extent: comeback, circumstances, and clock.

To start, there was the disparity in the teams' regular-season records. The Oilers finished 48 points ahead of the Kings in the standings. And the Oilers scored 417 goals (an

NHL record) to the Kings' 314. The Kings had beaten the Oilers only once in eight games during the regular season.

The Kings really had no business winning any games against the Oilers in their best-of-five series, but they had somehow taken the opener to gain a split of the first two games, played in Edmonton.

They certainly should not have won Game 3 after falling behind 5–0 in the first two periods back home at the Forum. The situation looked so bleak that Jerry Buss, who owned the Kings at the time, left and hopped in the limousine. He would be halfway to Palm Springs when the greatest comeback in Los Angeles history took place.

Five goals are much tougher to come by than three touchdowns, especially with only 20 minutes of hockey left to play.

But the Kings scored less than three minutes into the third period on a long shot by Jaw Wells. Then the Kings got a power play goal less than three minutes later. The Kings got a break on their third goal, when Oilers defenseman Randy Gregg accidentally knocked goaltender Grant Fuhr off the puck, allowing the puck to cross the goal line and make it 5–3.

Defenseman Mark Hardy made it 5–4 while the teams skated four-on-four.

But the Kings didn't get the tying goal until only five seconds remained, when Steve Bozek beat Grant Fuhr off a loose rebound. Overtime!

Two and a half minutes into the sudden-death period,

Daryl Evans whacked a slap shot past Fuhr, and the Kings had the improbable victory.

It set the standard for the largest deficit overcome in NHL history. But it wouldn't have meant much if the Kings didn't win the series.

Somehow, the Oilers shook off the devastating defeat and won Game 4. But the realization that the series should have already been over must have weighed on them on the flight back to Edmonton for Game 5. The Kings beat the Oilers in Game 5 to take the series and put a winning postscript on this city's greatest comeback victory.

WHO IS L.A.'S BIGGEST VILLAIN?

If sports are society's fastest factory for producing heroes, it makes sense that there have to be villains as well.

If you think about it, two thirds of sports energy is used for venting or booing: Cheer the home team, boo the officials, boo the opponent.

Los Angeles fans don't hate opponents just because they're good against their teams. For example, Lakers fans could always appreciate Julius Erving's grace or Michael Jordan's breath-taking flights.

It takes a special combination of attitude, jersey colors, and, yes, performance to get to be Public Enemy No. 1 in Los Angeles.

Danny Ainge had that mischievous face and played for the hated Boston Celtics. But he averaged only 4.8 points per game in the playoffs the year his Celtics beat the Lakers in the NBA finals. Larry Bird, Robert Parish, Kevin McHale, and Dennis Johnson did most of the damage. Ainge was more of an annoyance than an antagonist.

We've established that the Kings have the city's most passionate fans, but one of their favorite targets of scorn, Wayne Gretzky, became a King and a city favorite. Another hated foe, Rob Blake, was a former King who became a King again and was forgiven for talking and pricing himself out of town in the first place.

If you want a real bad guy, look to the North: to the Bay Area, to Barry Bonds.

Bonds' place in the Los Angeles doghouse was sealed when he did "The Pirouette." In September of 1997, Bonds hit a home run to beat the Dodgers and cut the Dodgers' two-game divisional lead in half. That was bad enough—almost a Joe Morgan-level crime. It's what Bonds did right after swatting the homer that really rankled Dodgers fans, though. He did a quick little spin before he left the batter's box, then merrily trotted toward first as he made his way around the bases. (The fans were just as agitated that Dodgers pitchers didn't throw a retaliatory fastball at him the following game.)

It didn't help that he set the single-season home run record against the Dodgers on the final weekend of the 2001 season. More negative points for Bonds: he bumped Southern California native and former USC star Mark McGwire from the top spot.

Then came BALCO, followed by a series of articles in the *San Francisco Chronicle* by Mark Fainaru-Wada and Lance Williams, and finally, their book *Game of Shadows*. Everywhere you turned, there were mounting allegations that performance-enhancing drugs fueled Bonds' late-career power surge. Bonds became the face of baseball's

75

steroids shame. And he just happened to be wearing a San Francisco Giants uniform.

Now Dodgers fans not only had new reasons to dislike Bonds, they had new derivative chants to yell at him from the stands.

"Bar-roid. Bar-roid."

Los Angeles fans generally avoid throwing things on the field, but if anyone brings out the hidden javelin-tossers in Dodgers fans, it's Bonds.

And one of the greatest signs of the extent of their hatred for Bonds came when he wasn't even in the building. When the Dodgers celebrated the 60th anniversary of Jackie Robinson's integration of Major League Baseball in 2007, Henry Aaron was on hand for the ceremonies.

Aaron's reign as the all-time home run champion had a dwindling life span, thanks to Bonds' hot pursuit. And Aaron had made it clear that, in his mind, Bonds' efforts were tainted. Any enemy of Bonds was an ally to Dodgers fans.

So that day at Dodger Stadium, Aaron's introduction drew some of the loudest cheers of the day. In addition, it drew a special chant: "Barry sucks."

WHAT WAS THE MOST COSTLY COACHING/MANAGING DECISION IN L.A. HISTORY?

The problem with managing or coaching is that the jobs look a lot easier than making a 25-foot jump shot or hitting a 99-mile-an-hour fastball. Most fans aren't delusional enough to think they could outperform elite athletes. But every fan thinks he could do a better job when it comes to making the critical decisions.

Would the typical fan be willing to face the criticism? Would he be able to make rational decisions under pressure? Sure, Tommy Lasorda's decision to send a hobbling Kirk Gibson to the plate in 1988 seems easy now, but what would we have said if Gibson struck out?

So we'll acknowledge and even admire those who make the calls under duress. But we must hold them accountable as well.

For all of Pat Riley's motivational triumphs, there is one tactical error he made that might have cost him untold amounts of money in selling Lakers "three-peat" shirts after he had the foresight to copyright the phrase.

It was 1989 and the Lakers, back-to-back defending champs, had breezed through the entire Western Conference playoffs. They looked as strong as ever, sweeping Portland, Seattle, and Phoenix. It turned out they were too efficient for their own good. Because they finished the Western Conference finals so early, while the Detroit Pistons went six games with the Chicago Bulls in the Eastern Conference finals, the Lakers had eight days off before the NBA finals began.

Riley was afraid of complacency and didn't want the Lakers to lose their edge. So he took them up to Santa Barbara and held training camp all over again. There were two-a-day workouts, and no mercy.

It's one thing to do that in October, when the players need to get back to game speed and top shape. It's another to do it after eight months and 93 games. Their bodies needed a break. Instead, Riley broke them. Byron Scott tore a hamstring and wound up missing the finals. Then Magic Johnson injured his hamstring during Game 2.

Scott had averaged 19.9 points per game in the playoffs that season, his highest playoff scoring average in his career. All the Lakers needed was an extra five points per game. They lost the first game by two points, the second by three points, and the third by four, in what turned out to be a Pistons sweep.

Riley wanted to keep things the same, but instead he caused a drastic change. Sometimes the enemy comes from within. It isn't easy to turn a juggernaut into a patsy, even before facing an opponent.

We'll let Riley off the hook because there was one even more notorious decision made four years earlier: Tommy Lasorda's decision to pitch to Jack Clark in Game 6 of the 1985 National League championship series.

The goat of that game turned out to be Tom Niedenfuer, but if part of a manager's job is to put his players in position to win, then Lasorda failed in this instance.

Niedenfuer came in during the seventh inning. This was before the era of superspecialization, when a closer had to get more than three outs. The Cardinals tied the score at 4–4, but the Dodgers went ahead in the bottom of the eighth inning on a home run by Mike Marshall.

Niedenfuer needed only three more outs for the Dodgers, who trailed 3–2 in the series, to force a Game 7.

In Game 5, two days earlier, Niedenfuer had served up a game-winning home run to Ozzie Smith. The switch-hitting Smith had never hit a home run from the left side of the plate before that one. Now Niedenfuer had a chance at redemption.

He struck out Cesar Cedeno. Willie McGee singled, then stole second, so the Dodgers walked Ozzie Smith to keep the double play in order. Tommy Herr grounded out, so now it was runners at second and third, two outs.

That brought Jack Clark to the plate, with first base empty. He didn't have his best season that year, with 22 home runs and 87 RBI in 126 games. But he was still a dangerous hitter in the prime of his career. He finished in the top 10 in National League home runs five times in the 1980s. And his bat was hot in that series; he had seven hits in 20 at-bats as he stepped to the plate. That 20 was significant: Clark averaged one home run every 20.1 at-bats that season. He hadn't hit one in the series yet. Talk about due; why tempt the numbers? Why not just walk him, especially when the man in the on-deck circle, Andy Van Slyke, was one for 10?

But Lasorda decided to stick with what he'd just seen. Niedenfuer had struck out Clark in the seventh inning.

But that was two innings earlier, and Clark was back on track. He whacked a Niedenfuer fastball into the Dodgers' bullpen beyond left field. The ball was hit so hard, its outcome so certain, that outfielder Pedro Guerrero didn't even bother to pursue it. He just slammed his glove to the field as the home run flew high above his head.

The Cardinals won the series. Lasorda won a spot in infamy.

WHO WAS THE GREATEST CHARACTER IN LOS ANGELES SPORTS?

23 Los Angeles has had plenty of personalities over the years, such as the charismatic Magic Johnson and the extroverted Tommy Lasorda. What it's lacked has been an abundance of characters, people who added a little comic relief to the proceedings for a town that can take its sports seriously. For a place with a laid-back reputation, there's a lot of pressure to do well. Los Angeles demands excellence and wastes no time with losers.

Every court needs a jester, and Los Angeles had its version with Jay Johnstone. He played in only 208 games with the Dodgers over the course of four different seasons, but that was enough time to establish his place in L.A. sports history. Besides, it's what he did off the field that set him apart.

It seemed you couldn't hear Johnstone's name without hearing the description "flake." It's surprising that wasn't listed as his position on his baseball card. But he worked hard for that reputation, earning it with a series of pranks and hijinks.

He went beyond the standard hotfoots in the dugout. The antithesis of the clean and proper Steve Garvey, Johnstone once stuck a brownie in Garvey's first baseman's glove. He ran a pair of relief pitcher Steve Howe's underwear up a flag pole. Not even the manager, Lasorda, was granted immunity from Johnstone's antics. Johnstone once took the pictures of celebrities that hung on Lasorda's office wall and replaced them with pictures of himself and pitchers Jerry Reuss and Don Stanhouse. Another time, Johnstone trapped Lasorda in his room during spring training, then disabled the phone so Lasorda couldn't call for help.

Johnstone wasn't all about making others look bad. He could have some fun at his own expense as well. He once stood in line at the concessions stand during a game—while wearing his uniform. Another time, he joined the grounds crew and swept the infield between innings.

Johnstone could play a little baseball. He was good enough to last for 20 years in the major leagues after breaking in with the Angels in 1966. He batted .267 and hit 102 home runs over his career. He was with the Dodgers from 1980–82, then joined the Chicago Cubs, and came back to the Dodgers for his final season in 1985.

The Dodgers used him primarily as a pinch-hitter, and in that role he had a big part in their 1981 championship. He was 11 for 38 with three home runs as a pinch-hitter, and his two-run home run sparked a Dodgers comeback in Game 4 of the World Series.

But when Dodgers fans think of Johnstone, hitting heroics is not the first thing that comes to mind.

It's the screwy stories, such as this one Johnstone told the *Chicago Sun-Times* in 2001: "I couldn't give a urine sample in spring training in Dodgertown in Vero Beach, Fla., because Steve Yeager and I went out partying every night and all I wanted in the morning was coffee and doughnuts. You can't give a true sample with that stuff in your body. Tommy Lasorda threatened to fine me, but I went out with Yeager and his buddies again, and that meant more coffee and doughnuts. I grabbed an apple juice, poured it into a sample jar and took it into a Nurse Ratchet-type lady, who held it up and said, `My, my, Mr. Johnstone, we're a little cloudy today, aren't we?' Seeing three rookies there, I took the jar back and said, `You're right,' and drank the whole thing."

This was the sign of someone who was being a flake just for the sake of being flaky, not an attention-seeking eccentric hoping to cash in on his alter ego. The Lakers had that with Dennis Rodman, who had become a self-parody by the time he arrived for a short-lived stay in 1999.

BASKETBALL

WHO IS THE LAKERS' GREATEST COACH?

 24 Bill Sharman won the most single-season games in franchise history with the 1971–72 squad, but it takes multiple titles to enter this argument.

Yes, Pat Riley won more championships than Phil Jackson as a Lakers coach (4–3). But his achievements are diminished just slightly because Paul Westhead won a championship with the Magic–Kareem tandem before Riley, and Mike Dunleavy reached the NBA finals with Magic after Riley. Shaquille O'Neal and Kobe Bryant never made it out of the Western Conference before Phil Jackson coached them. And Kobe and company missed the playoffs entirely the first year Jackson was gone.

Riley actually peaked as a coach after he left the Lakers. He reinvented himself with the New York Knicks, adapting his style to a less talented team, ditching "Showtime" in favor of what he dubbed "force" basketball. It wasn't as pretty to watch (a downgrade from ballet to slam-dancing), but his players all bought into it and the Knicks came within a game of winning a championship in 1994. Riley has spent 14 years coaching the Knicks and the Miami Heat, long ago surpassing the nine he spent with the Lakers.

Jackson's NBA coaching career has almost been evenly split between the Lakers and Chicago Bulls. In Chicago he had a more mature team, one with a savvier basketball IQ. Jackson had younger, more distracted, less cooperative superstars in Bryant and O'Neal. But he got them to coexist long enough to win three consecutive championships. And given what we now know about all the chaos that went on in 2004, it's a miracle that team even reached the NBA finals. Jackson's coaching job that year was actually underrated.

Riley created a sense of urgency every night of the season. A January game in Cleveland meant just as much to him as a playoff Game 7. Jackson took the opposite approach, never panicking during a bad stretch in a game, or a few bad outings during the regular season. He took a bigger-picture view—a more holistic, Zen approach, if you will—and eventually his players grasped the concept. They were at their best in the postseason, when it mattered most. Jackson's teams never wore out, they peaked—just as Jackson reached his pinnacle at the end of his career, with the Lakers. It was a run that surpassed the performance of everyone who held the job before him.

WHAT WAS KOBE BRYANT'S GREATEST PERFORMANCE?

Ask most people to name Kobe Bryant's greatest NBA accomplishment and they'll say it was his 81-point game against Toronto in 2006. They couldn't be more wrong.

Eighty-one is just a number, a mathematical accomplishment. It really didn't mean anything. It was the most points ever scored by a Laker, but it wasn't an NBA record. In the long run, what was accomplished? The Lakers beat a woeful Toronto Raptors team during the regular season.

Bryant has played so many games that meant so much more, come through so many times when his best was required, that the 81-point night isn't even close to his best.

If anything, watching him single-handedly outscore the Dallas Mavericks, 62–61, through three quarters earlier in the 2005–06 season was more impressive because it came against a better team. But that still wasn't his best.

Kobe's two biggest moments produced less gaudy statistics…but they did result in a set of oversized diamond rings. It was all about the circumstances, which is how 8 points can trump 81. On June 14, 2000, the Lakers found themselves tied with the Indiana Pacers after four quarters had ended in Game 4 of the NBA finals. If they weren't careful, they soon could have found themselves tied in the series as well.

All Bryant did was score eight points in the overtime period. He did it despite a sprained ankle that had kept him out of Game 3. The moment was there, and he grabbed it. There had been plenty of times when there had been comparisons made between Bryant and Michael Jordan. Suddenly it seemed worthwhile to do so.

Years later, Bryant would look back and say, "That was the coming out party. That was the beginning. People had to step back and say, 'This kid is for real.'"

But that moment never would have arrived had it not been for Bryant's performance 10 days earlier. In Game 7 of the Western Conference finals, the Lakers overcame a 15-point deficit in the fourth quarter and rallied to beat the Portland Trail Blazers. Bryant was the driving force behind it all.

He led the Lakers in every major statistical category: 25 points, 11 rebounds, 7 assists, and 4 blocked shots.

The Lakers became so dominant over the next couple of years, it's easy to forget how fragile they were at the start, how it could have ended before it even began. Bryant, only 21 years old at the time, made sure it didn't happen.

Although the Lakers had tremendous talent and were the best team in the league that year, they were still learning how to win. They hadn't been there before.

If it hadn't happened at that juncture, they may never have gotten there again. There was always an underlying tension between Bryant and Shaquille O'Neal. It boiled over the next season, with a string of public sniping in the middle of the year. If they didn't have a championship to defend, the Lakers might have to consider scrapping the tandem before the team imploded. But with the memories of their championship parade still fresh in their heads, the Lakers decided to stick it out a while longer. It turned out to be two more championships longer. All thanks to that victory over Portland.

All thanks to Bryant.

"Portland is the one," he said. "We don't step up that game, you don't know what could have happened. It's the most important."

WHO WAS RESPONSIBLE FOR THE BREAKUP OF THE LAKERS IN 2004?

Sometimes the fate of the Lakers has been determined by such random acts as flips and flukes. There were the coin tosses that resulted in the draft position used to select Magic Johnson and James Worthy. There was Jack McKinney's bicycle accident that led to Paul Westhead replacing him as coach.

The Lakers breakup of 2004 didn't turn on a single moment like those. It unfolded gradually, with forces and agendas colliding like a Shakespearean play. All of the main tragic elements came into play: pride, greed, and lust. The result was yet another turn of fate, one that took the Lakers from a dominant team that aspired to be included among the NBA's great dynasties to a marginal ballclub that had to battle the long-downtrodden Clippers just for supremacy in its own building.

Perhaps trading Shaquille O'Neal to the Miami Heat didn't send the Lakers to "bolivion" (as Mike Tyson would say) or "expansionism" (to borrow a phrase O'Neal himself created). But it made them mediocre. Ordinary.

And in a market like Los Angeles, that's just as bad. To make it even worse for the Lakers, O'Neal won the race back to victory lane, winning a championship in his second season in Miami.

There's plenty of blame to go around, but one man deserves the biggest share. In reverse order of responsibility:

3. SHAQUILLE O'NEAL

He came into training camp before the 2004 season talking about a contract extension. Unfortunately, he didn't come into camp in top shape. But he was feeling frisky enough to turn a jumper and a blocked shot on back-to-back plays in an exhibition game into proof (in his mind) that he deserved another $30 million per year. He yelled a few choice words—the printable part included the words "pay me"—at Lakers owner Jerry Buss, who was sitting courtside. Before the next exhibition game the following night, O'Neal walked by a group of reporters, rubbed his fingers together, and said, "Show me the money!"

O'Neal kept saying he wouldn't take a "drastic drop" in salary, as Kevin Garnett had when extending what had been the NBA's richest contract when he re-upped with the Minnesota Timberwolves. To top it off, O'Neal missed 15 games that season with an assortment of injuries, and that didn't help Buss forget the 2002–03 season, when O'Neal waited until right before training camp to have toe surgery.

Still, when it mattered most, O'Neal could perform like

no other center in the game. In the Lakers' five-game loss to the Detroit Piston in the 2004 NBA finals, O'Neal averaged 26.6 points, 10.8 rebounds, and made more than 60 percent of his shots. And as it turned out, money was not that big of an issue, and the numbers weren't as large as the figures that made Buss balk. When it came time to negotiate with Miami a year later, O'Neal wound up signing for an average of $20 million a year. Still plenty of money, but compared to what he had been making—and seeking—it might actually qualify as a drastic drop.

2. KOBE BRYANT

For an event that was never proven to be a crime, Kobe Bryant's extramarital affair in Colorado in the summer of 2003 sure meted out punishment. There was the loss of millions in endorsement dollars to Bryant, and in a real sense it probably cost the Lakers any shot at reconciling the rocky relationship between Bryant and O'Neal. O'Neal got word that Bryant had used Shaq as an example of a philandering superstar when the police interviewed Bryant. So it's no surprise that O'Neal never strongly supported Kobe during Bryant's legal ordeal. They both retreated to their corners while Phil Jackson, unsure of how to approach Bryant during those touchy times, made no attempt to bring them together.

During Bryant's "Trade me—or not" summer of 2007, he insisted that Lakers owner Jerry Buss had told him in

February of 2004 that he didn't want to pay O'Neal, so he would trade him while he could still get value in return.

Where Bryant is culpable is that he never tried to talk Buss out of it. For all of their differences, Bryant and O'Neal still made for an almost unstoppable tandem: four trips to the NBA finals in five years and three championship parades. But Bryant didn't want to just be part of a tandem like Lewis and Clark. He yearned to be the sole leader, Edmund Hillary scaling to the top of Mt. Everest first.

Had Bryant gone to Buss and told him they needed to keep O'Neal to have another shot at a championship, Buss would have had to acquiesce. Buss was determined to do whatever he could to keep Bryant—a pending free agent—happy and in a Lakers uniform.

But Bryant wanted to try things his own way. According to Jackson's *The Last Season*, when he asked Bryant if O'Neal's presence would affect his decision to come back or not, Bryant said, "Yes, it does," and later adding, "I'm tired of being a sidekick."

He was a sidekick no more. Just the captain of a ship stuck in the harbor.

1. JERRY BUSS

If Kobe Bryant is the captain, Jerry Buss is the fleet commander. Ultimately everything was his decision—and in this case, his mistake.

He had O'Neal under contract for one more year (through

2004–05) before O'Neal could opt out. But under the NBA's salary cap rules, O'Neal could not make as much money signing elsewhere as he could if he stayed with the Lakers. And if he wanted to make as much money as possible, Buss could have suggested, he might want to shed some pounds.

The same salary cap rules applied to Bryant. He would have to walk away from an extra $30 million, guaranteed, if he signed anywhere else. Remember, this was at a time when he had lost millions of dollars in endorsements because of the sexual assault allegation, and the case against him had not yet been dropped.

Buss, a serious poker player, folded.

He didn't hang in to force O'Neal to sign for less. He did not dare Bryant to give up $30 million.

He had already lost the greatest general manager of his generation, when Jerry West left after the 2000 season. Now in the span of less than four weeks, he traded away the greatest center of his time, and parted ways with the greatest coach of his time.

The bitter irony is that he did not wind up saving money. He let Jackson go and committed $20 million to Rudy Tomjanovich, only to have Tomjanovich quit during his first season and Jackson come back the next year at $10 million per. And the Lakers had to take on Brian Grant's bulky contract as part of the O'Neal trade. Even though the Lakers waived Grant after one season, they still had to pay him $17 million in 2006–07. That was only $3 million less than

O'Neal. Factor in the revenue missing from the extra playoff games O'Neal could have brought to Staples Center, and Buss probably lost money on the whole exchange.

That makes him the biggest loser in this sorry affair.

WHAT UNSUNG LAKERS HERO SHOULD HAVE HIS JERSEY RETIRED?

It takes more than movie stars to make a successful motion picture. You need screenwriters and location scouts, set constructors, sound technicians, and stunt doubles, too.

Magic Johnson, Kareem Abdul-Jabbar, and James Worthy made the marquee during the Lakers' "Showtime" days. Michael Cooper was the guy working behind the camera.

On a team known for its flashy, high-powered offense, Cooper's specialty was defense. He guarded the other team's best players at a variety of positions. He might have to defend superquick point guard Isiah Thomas of the Detroit Pistons one night and lethal shooting guard Michael Jordan of the Chicago Bulls the next night. Or he could find himself going against Larry Bird in the Boston Garden.

Cooper played on all five Lakers championship teams in the 1980s. Those five rings were as many as Magic and George Mikan own, to name two all-time Lakers greats. Only 13 players in NBA history have more rings than Coop. Eight of those players are already in the Hall of Fame and two more (Michael Jordan and Scottie Pippen) are on their way.

That's not to say Cooper should be in the hoop hall in Springfield, Massachusetts, but they should at least hang his No. 21 from the wall in Staples Center.

It would be a fitting reward for a career-long Laker and someone who went on to serve the organization by coaching the WNBA's Sparks to a pair of championships.

He ought to have his own time at center stage, with all eyes on him.

Cooper didn't get introduced to run on to the court and high-five his teammates before the game because he usually wasn't in the starting lineup. He came off the bench for the majority of the 873 games he played with the Lakers from 1978–1990. His name wasn't called in the first round of the draft, either. The Lakers took him with the 16th pick in the third round, 60th overall, in 1978. The third round of the draft doesn't even exist anymore. (Coincidentally, the third round of the 1978 draft also brought in two players who would be Cooper-like supplementary parts for the Lakers' rivals Boston and Philadelphia in the 1980s: Gerald Henderson and Marc Iavaroni.)

Cooper found his niche, realizing that defense was his way to stay in the league, and he played it so well that in 1986–87 he became the first (and still only) Laker to win the Defensive Player of the Year award.

And has there ever been a Laker with such a unique way of dressing on the court? Cooper kept his socks pulled up to his knees long after it was fashionable (and before ballers from Washington, D.C., brought it back). He wore his drawstrings dangling down the front of his shorts and had thick wristbands reminiscent of Space Ghost.

He also had his signature play: the Coop-a-loop, when Norm Nixon or Magic Johnson would throw Cooper a lob pass that he'd slam home.

Cooper developed into a pretty good outside shooter, and in 1986–87 he finished eighth in the league in three-point shooting, making 38.5 percent of his shots from behind the arc.

His most memorable shot came when he hit a jumper to win Game 5 of the 1988 conference semifinals against Utah. It was the pivotal game of the series that was surprisingly tough for them. Without Cooper's shot it was quite possible that the Lakers would have had to go to Utah, down three games to two, to play Game 6. Instead they absorbed the loss in Salt Lake City, came home to triumph in Game 7, and went on to claim back-to-back championships.

Cooper is in the Lakers' all-time top 10 in three-point field goal shooting, free throw percentage, minutes played, assists, steals, and blocked shots.

The fans used to flood the Forum with chants of "Cooooooooop."

They recognized his value to the team. The Lakers should, too.

WHO WOULD YOU RATHER HAVE TAKE THE LAST SHOT, JERRY WEST OR KOBE BRYANT?

You're coaching the 12 greatest Lakers players of all time. There are 10 seconds left in the game and you're down by one point. Which player gets the ball in the play you diagram?

Would it be the man they call "Mr. Clutch?"

He did shoot 47 percent for his career, and shot 48 percent or better in five of his 13 seasons. Bryant never shot 48 percent in his first 11 seasons in the NBA.

Two of West's noted plays were a steal and layup on the last play of Game 3 of the 1962 NBA finals to beat the Boston Celtics, 117–115. He also hit a jumper from the corner in Game 1 of the 1973 Western Conference finals against Golden State.

And if you needed a 60-foot shot, West was your man. His buzzer-beater against the Knicks at the end of regulation in Game 3 of the 1970 NBA finals remains one of the most famous shots in NBA history. After a New York free throw gave the Knicks a two-point lead with three seconds left, West calmly took the inbounds pass, dribbled twice to get past the top of the key in the backcourt, then let it fly—nothing but net. A forgotten postscript: The Lakers lost the game...and the series.

Indeed, for all of West's postseason brilliance—he set records for playoff points and scoring average—he only cashed in once in nine trips to the NBA finals.

Bryant had three championships, and made at least one game-winning shot along the road in each of them. In 2000 there was a buzzer-beater in Game 2 of the second round against Phoenix and an eight-point overtime outburst in Game 4 of the NBA finals against Indiana. In 2001 there was a put-back to win Game 1 and a three-pointer to win Game 2 of the Western Conference finals against San Antonio. And in 2002 he hit a jumper against the New Jersey Nets to give the Lakers a 3–0 lead in the NBA finals.

Bryant can match West clutch shot for clutch shot. But West couldn't duplicate Bryant's athleticism, which gives Bryant the ability to create shots when none appear to be available. They might not be what the coach draws up in the huddle. They might not be recommended for mere mortals. They sometimes don't even qualify as good shots. But Bryant might be the best bad-shot maker in the history of the league.

Bryant's two plays in the final game of the 2003–04 regular season serve as examples 1 and 1A of his ability.

The Pacific Division championship was there for the taking after a surprising Sacramento loss to Golden State

101

that night. But the Lakers looked ready to squander it against the Portland Trail Blazers.

With the Lakers down by three points and eight seconds remaining in the fourth quarter, Portland defended the three-point arc. Ruben Patterson, the self-proclaimed Kobe-stopper, guarded Bryant.

Bryant dribbled to his right, crossed over to his left hand, but couldn't shake Patterson. He pump faked, but Patterson didn't buy it and held his ground, his hands straight up like a robber's victim. Bryant created a little wiggle room, jumping to his left and shooting the ball at the hoop as his body veered toward the sideline. Swish. Overtime.

In overtime, the Lakers were down by two points with one second remaining. Bryant came toward the sidelines to take an inbounds pass from Gary Payton. In one move—and in less than one second—Bryant caught the ball, turned toward the hoop, and let a three-pointer fly over the outstretched arms of the 6-foot-10 Theo Ratliff. By the time the ball completed its 23-foot arc and dropped through the net, the Lakers were Pacific Division champs.

You can't find an example of a player making two more difficult, important shots in the same game. And you can't find a better clutch shooter than Bryant. That's why, given the choice of any Laker in history, Bryant should get the ball with the game on the line.

WHAT WAS JERRY WEST'S WORST MOVE?

29 It's easy to catalog Jerry West's triumphs as a Lakers executive. He could go to the personnel Hall of Fame just for the summer when he brought in Shaquille O'Neal and Kobe Bryant. In fact, you could argue he did more for the team in the front office than he did on the court.

But even the best can mess up. After all, Steven Spielberg directed *Hook*. Bruce Springsteen released a dance remix to "Dancing in the Dark."

For most of his career, West kept coming up with gold in every stream he searched. It didn't matter that the Lakers' success meant they usually drafted near the end of the first round. He could find the likes of A. C. Green with the 23rd pick. And he had an uncanny knack for picking up the right pieces as the season went on. His midseason acquisition of Mychal Thompson in 1987 was the final step that enabled them to win back-to-back championships.

But sometimes West's good steps merely served to mask his bad steps. West received another round of kudos in 1993 when he grabbed Nick Van Exel—a future All-Star— in the second round with the 37th overall pick. People overlooked his first-round pick that year, the undersized power forward George Lynch at No. 12. West passed on Sam Cassell, who proved to be a more stable point guard than the volatile Van Exel. Cassell won two championships with the Houston Rockets.

At least Van Exel was a positive part of the "Lake Show" squads that revived the team in the mid-1990s and made the team an appealing destination when O'Neal hit free agency. If that group didn't look like a promising team, it's doubtful O'Neal would have risked leaving the talented nucleus of the Orlando Magic to come to L.A.

However, one of the reasons the Lakers needed to be revived in the first place, the trap door that caused them to tumble down into the pit, was West's worst trade.

It happened on February 22, 1993, when West traded Sam Perkins to the Seattle SuperSonics for Benoit Benjamin and Doug Christie. Yes, this was the same Benoit Benjamin that slothed his way through five uninspired seasons with the Clippers.

The Lakers were 26–23 at the time of the trade. They finished 39–43 (although that was good enough to make the playoffs in a depleted Western Conference). Benjamin did nothing to reward West's gamble, averaging 4.5 points during his short stay in purple and gold. That summer the Lakers traded him to New Jersey for Sam Bowie and a second-round pick.

Perkins was an undervalued asset that the Lakers shipped out for too little in return. At the time, he had delivered the franchise's last NBA finals game victory, when he drilled a three-pointer to win Game 1 against the Chicago Bulls in 1991. Perkins would go on to play in the finals two more times: with the Seattle SuperSonics in 1996 and with the Indiana Pacers in 2000. Perkins had four more seasons of double-digit scoring in him after the Lakers traded him.

Meanwhile, things really bottomed out for the Lakers the next season. They finished 33–49 and missed the playoffs for the first time in 18 years. It cost Randy Pfund his job as coach, and led to the ill-fated experiment of Magic Johnson as coach. The only good thing to come out of that disastrous year was the Lakers got the No. 10 pick in the draft. West used it on Eddie Jones. The Lakers—and West—were on their way back to restoring their good names.

WHO ARE THE ALL-TIME BEST LAKERS?

POINT GUARD: MAGIC JOHNSON

At point guard, Magic Johnson is a no-brainer. He'd be in the starting backcourt with Michael Jordan for the all-time NBA team. But if you insist on seeing the credentials (kind of like a bouncer carding a man with gray hair), here you go: five-time NBA champion, played in the NBA finals 8 of his first 10 seasons in the league, three-time MVP of the regular season, three-time finals MVP, held career assists record, and still holds records for career assists-per-game and most playoff assists.

Oh, and he's *Magic Johnson*.

People forget that Norm Nixon used to run the point before Johnson got there, and they shared the position during Magic's first three seasons in L.A. Often, the point guard was determined by whoever got to the ball first. It worked well enough to win two championships for the Lakers...until the Lakers traded Nixon to the Clippers for Byron Scott.

31 SHOOTING GUARD: JERRY WEST

His running mate in the backcourt is much more difficult. For now, Jerry West's accomplishments win out over Kobe Bryant's talent.

West is the Lakers' all-time scoring leader, with 25,192 points. You can't have an all-franchise team without the team's all-time scorer. Even if you go by averages, to account for West's longer career, it's still West with the edge in scoring (27.0 to 24.6), assists (6.7 to 4.5), and shooting percentage (47 percent to 45 percent).

Is Bryant being penalized for playing alongside Shaquille O'Neal in the prime of O'Neal's career? Let's not forget, West played alongside a dominant center in Wilt Chamberlain. This might not have been the 50-point-per-game Wilt of 1962, but Chamberlain was coming off an MVP season when he joined the Lakers in 1968–69. That year, West led the squad in scoring with a 25.9 per game average; Chamberlain was at 20.5. Elgin Baylor averaged 24.8—which brings up another point. West played along Baylor for the first 10 seasons of his career and with Chamberlain for the final five (two full years with both). So for his entire career West played with at least one of the game's all-time great scorers, whereas Bryant hasn't had to share the ball, or scoring duties, with anyone of that magnitude during his points explosion since Shaq was traded to Miami in 2004. And West had as many appearances on the NBA's all-defensive first team as Bryant (four).

FORWARD: ELGIN BAYLOR

Elgin Baylor is another easy choice. He's third in the franchise in scoring and still holds the NBA finals record for points in a game (61). Bryant had to pass Baylor to get to most of his spots in the Lakers scoring record book. Baylor also took the game off the ground and turned it into the aerial ballet it became in the 1980s.

The one knock against Baylor was that he never won a championship. He had the misfortune of retiring at the start of the 1971–72 season, which the Lakers turned into one of the best in NBA history and resulted in their first championship in Los Angeles.

In distant second place here is Jamaal Wilkes, a member of the Lakers' championship teams in 1980, 1982, and 1985. (For what it's worth, Wilkes also won a championship with the Golden State Warriors.) "Silk" had that funny-looking windup to his jump shot, but they went in with such regularity that announcer Chick Hearn used to call them "20-foot layups." Wilkes' 10,601 points are 10th all-time on the Lakers list.

FORWARD: JAMES WORTHY

The other forward is not as simple as it might seem. Sure, James Worthy is a Hall of Famer and the MVP of the 1988 NBA finals. "Showtime" would not have been the same without his swooping one-handed dunks to finish off the fast break. But wouldn't a team need a physical presence at the power forward spot? A. C. Green did grab 5,632 rebounds as a Laker, enough to put him in the franchise's top 10 (and ahead of another forward candidate, Happy Hairston). But it's just too hard to pass on Worthy, who is in the Lakers' top 10 in points, field goals, field goal percentage, free throws made, assists, steals, and blocked shots. Besides, he was considered a power forward when he first came in the league; he just wound up a better fit as a small forward. We'll move him back to make room for him—and let others worry about how to match up with his quickness.

CENTER: KAREEM ABDUL-JABBAR

The Lakers' center spot is the most loaded position of any team in the NBA. Three all-time greats representing three eras (and that doesn't even include George Mikan, a Laker when the franchise was in Minneapolis).

How to choose between Wilt Chamberlain, Kareem Abdul-Jabbar, and Shaquille O'Neal? It comes down to consistency.

Chamberlain came to the Lakers on the downside of his record-setting career. His five years in L.A. produced his five lowest season point totals, including one year in which he played in only 12 games. He did average over 18 rebounds in four of the years. He was great, but he wasn't at his greatest.

O'Neal's MVP season of 1999–2000 was a sight to

109

behold. He averaged 29.7 points, 13.6 rebounds, 3.8 assists, and 3 blocks per game, and for a while the Lakers made a run at the team-best 69 victories established by the Chamberlain–West squad in 1971–72. But he never played in more than 67 games in his final three seasons in Los Angeles, before his time with the Lakers came to a premature end. Had he retired as a Laker, perhaps this order would be different.

But we're honoring longevity, along with productivity. Kareem had one truly dominant year, his first in Los Angeles after the Milwaukee Bucks shipped him west in exchange for four players. In 1975–76 Abdul-Jabbar averaged 27.7 points, 16.9 rebounds, 5 assists, and 4.1 blocked shots. Abdul-Jabbar averaged at least 21 points per game in 11 of his 14 seasons as a Laker. He was there for all five championships in the 1980s, giving the Lakers a reliable scoring option in the half-court offense whenever they weren't running the fast break. And as a career 72 percent free-throw shooter (both Chamberlain and O'Neal shot in the 50s), Abdul-Jabbar also could be trusted at the line at the end of close games, including the important free throws he made in Game 6 of the 1988 NBA finals.

WHAT WAS THE WORST CLIPPERS DRAFT DAY?

35 Going through the Clippers' draft picks over the years is always good for a laugh ... unless you're a hard-core Clippers fan. Then it's like hitting your hand with a hammer again and again and again.

Any team can make a mistake on draft day. But to keep blowing it year after year takes a remarkable combination of bad scouting, bad decisions, and even bad breaks. Trying to sort through the blunders to find the worst one is just as challenging.

How about Chris Wilcox over Amare Stoudemire in 2002? Or Shaun Livingston over Luol Deng in 2004?

Not even close.

Lancaster Gordon over John Stockton in 1984?

Michael Olowokandi over Mike Bibby, Vince Carter, Dirk Nowitzki, and Paul Pierce in 1998?

That's getting to the proper threshold of pain, but nowhere near as bad as 1987. That was the year the Clippers had three first-round picks, but somehow did not use any of them to take: Scottie Pippen, Reggie Miller, Horace Grant, Mark Jackson, Kevin Johnson, or Kenny Smith.

The Clippers wound up with Reggie Williams, Joe Wolf, and Ken Norman.

With the No. 4 pick the Clippers could have selected Pippen, who redefined the forward position and became the NBA's ultimate shotgun rider next to Michael Jordan. Or they could have had Miller, who became the NBA's greatest three-point shooter. They could have chosen Horace Grant, the hard-working forward who became an All-Star and a four-time NBA champion. Or either of the two quick point guards, Smith or Johnson.

Instead they chose Reggie Williams, the slender guard from Georgetown who averaged 10 points a game over three seasons with the Clippers.

When it was time for the 13th pick, Jackson was still on the board. Little did the Clippers know Jackson was about to become the Rookie of the Year, or that he'd go on to dish off more assists than Magic Johnson.

They took Joe Wolf. North Carolina products who played for Dean Smith tended to do well in the NBA. Wolf didn't follow the pattern, unless 5.8 points a game for three years is what you're looking for in a first-round pick.

You know the saddest thing? Not only did the other teams manage to find better players that the Clippers passed over, but even the *Clippers* found a better player that they passed over with their first two picks.

Ken Norman, whom the Clippers selected at No. 19, was actually a pretty good player. He sure was more productive than their first two picks. He stayed with the Clippers twice as long as the other two players, and wound up scoring three times as many points for the Clippers as the other two combined.

So the Clippers got a solid starter. But they passed on six players who started for teams that played in the NBA finals. Two of them—Pippen and Miller—are headed to the Hall of Fame.

The Clippers keep heading back to the draft lottery...and we've seen what that does for them.

WHICH CLIPPER SHOULD BE THE FIRST TO HAVE HIS NAME RAISED TO THE RAFTERS?

If you walk into Staples Center on a night when the Clippers aren't playing, there's no evidence that they even occupy the building.

The Lakers, the Kings, the Sparks...even the Avengers of the Arena Football League have retired numbers and championship banners of some type hanging high on the western wall to commemorate the accomplishments of their teams and players.

The Clippers don't even have a patch.

They have been famous for their futility ever since they arrived in Los Angeles from San Diego in 1984. They're closing in on 2 ½ decades without so much as a division title.

And while they have had former players go on to the basketball Hall of Fame, such as Bill Walton and Dominique Wilkins, they certainly weren't being honored for anything they did in a Clippers uniform.

In his first six seasons in Los Angeles, Elton Brand has certainly earned a spot in the Clippers' select circle. Brand already has more points and rebounds than any other L.A. Clippers player, and he led the team to its best season in franchise history when the Clippers went to the second round of the 2006 playoffs.

But his No. 42 can't be retired while he's still playing. The Clippers need something now, a reminder that they call Staples Center home as well. That's why there should be a tribute to Ralph Lawler.

The Lakers set the precedent for honoring a broadcaster when they hung a jersey with Chick Hearn's name and a microphone after Hearn died in 2002. Why wait until Lawler passes away?

He already has the credentials. He has called more than 2,000 Clippers games on television and radio.

He has the battle scars as well, having endured seasons of 12 and 15 victories. (That total doesn't even include the lockout-shortened 1999 season, when the Clippers won 9 out of 50 games.)

Somehow he has survived all of that bad basketball without going crazy. He's still optimistic.

And he still holds his microphone like a roving reporter, instead of using the headset microphone that became the play-by-play standard years ago.

Lawler is from Peoria, Illinois, the same city that gave us Chick Hearn. And he never complained about being over-shadowed by Hearn in this market for so many years.

Lawler has his own little cache of catch phrases, including "Bingo!" for a three-pointer, "Lawler's Law" (first team to score 100 points will win), and "Oh me, oh my" (which can be used in admiration, or, more often, frustration).

If the Clippers want to have their existence acknowledged, they should acknowledge Lawler's contributions.

WHAT'S THE BEST MOVE THE CLIPPERS EVER MADE?

Yes, even the Clippers get it right on occasion. Remember that day?

Ah yes, June 27, 2001.

That's the day they traded the draft rights to Tyson Chandler (along with forward Brian Skinner) to Chicago for Elton Brand.

Not only did they wind up with the best player in franchise history, they brought one of the NBA's best citizens to Los Angeles. The Clippers and the city were better off for it.

Better yet: Chandler has yet to average double-digit scoring in the NBA and no longer plays for the Bulls, making this the most lopsided trade in Clippers history.

What's not to like? Well, in typical Clippers tradition, the best isn't quite good enough. Brand is one of the better power forwards in the game, but he's still on a tier below the likes of Tim Duncan and Dirk Nowitzki.

But enough about what Brand isn't. What he is, is a guy who can get you 20 points and 10 rebounds on any given night—and be the media's go-to quote afterward. Plus he'd probably offer a fan a ride home if his car broke down in the parking lot.

It's hard to believe such a player was available at that point in his career, only two years out of Duke. What were the Bulls thinking? Actually, they were behaving a lot like the Clippers, who had been stockpiling young players who were on their rookie contract scales (and therefore, cheaper). Rather than deal with Brand's rookie contract expiring, the Bulls could reset the clock with Chandler and have him for four years before they had to worry about signing him to a big contract or losing him to free agency.

If there was a year to give up the second pick, it was 2001. It was a draft littered with unknowns. The top four picks consisted of three players straight out of high school, plus Pau Gasol of Spain (who wound up being the best of the bunch). Kwame Brown was selected first by the Washington Wizards with the No. 1 pick.

Los Angeles fans know how that turned out: He wound up being a disappointment with the Lakers after four disappointing seasons in Washington.

Sure, Chandler was intriguing. He was taller and more athletic than Brand. But could he play? Brand was a proven commodity, winning collegiate National Player of the Year awards at Duke, where he took the Blue Devils to the championship game. For the Bulls to get the better of the trade, Chandler would have to do better than Brand's 20 points and 10 rebounds per game. The only players to do that in the

2000–01 season were Chris Webber, Shaquille O'Neal, Tim Duncan, Kevin Garnett, and Antonio McDyess. The Clippers had already traded the draft rights to McDyess once before (for Rodney Rogers, no less). This time, they wouldn't be making the same mistake. Chandler was no McDyess. And he definitely wasn't a Webber, O'Neal, Duncan, or Garnett.

He wasn't even close to being Brand. No other Clipper is, either. Brand is the team's all-time scoring and rebounding leader. And in his long-awaited first trip to the playoffs, Brand performed like a battle-tested veteran, averaging 25 points, 10 rebounds, and 2.6 blocks per game while shooting 55 percent from the field.

And you couldn't find a better guy. He won the NBA's sportsmanship award in 2006. When he was still with the Bulls he won the Pro Basketball Writers Association's Magic Johnson Award for his work with the media and in the community.

Want an example of his generosity? At the 2007 Cedars-Sinai Sports Spectacular, a fund-raiser to help the hospital research and fight birth defects, Brand heard they had raised $1.9 million. He decided to make it an even $2 million by donating $100,000.

In this case there's nothing to question about the Clippers' choice...other than to wonder if they can get anyone else like him.

IS DONALD STERLING THE WORST OWNER IN PROFESSIONAL SPORTS HISTORY?

38 What makes Los Angeles so difficult is the comparisons. You might like your car, but there's always a chance a Ferrari could pull up next to you at the light and put you to shame. Perhaps you were a beauty queen back in Iowa, but in this town you're just another face at the open casting call.

Donald Sterling didn't help himself in the appearance category by moving the Clippers from San Diego to Los Angeles. The franchise that defined mediocrity now lived just down the street from what had become the standard of sporting excellence for a quarter of a century.

It started right away, when the Clippers arrived in 1984. The Lakers won 62 games and the NBA championship. The Clippers won 63 games—total—in their first two seasons in L.A. It got worse from there, as the Clippers won 12, then 17 games the next two seasons. Meanwhile, the Lakers eventually won six championships and went to the NBA finals an additional three times.

In the real world, Sterling was an American success story,

coming from nothing in East Los Angeles to run a legal and real estate empire. To sports fans he was a failure.

His team has been to the playoffs only four times, winning one series. It has been a place where careers go to die. Did you ever notice that "living in Los Angeles" always was an intangible side benefit to prospective Lakers free agents, but that advantage never seemed to apply to the Clippers? It was as if the dark cloud that hovered above the franchise loomed so large it could block out the Southern California sunshine. Of course it didn't help that Sterling didn't have a reputation for writing large checks to bring players in.

The Clippers habitually resided at the low end of the NBA's payroll scale, ranking last in the league for one four-year stretch and sometimes flirting with the league's team salary minimum. For those who played well enough to earn a big contract, it meant leaving town to sign it.

And there was one word of caution for the team's coaches: rent. Sterling went through 16 coaches in 25 years. One coach (Bill Fitch) had to sue Sterling just to get the money still owed to him on his contract after he was fired.

Sterling certainly qualifies for the all-time worst owner derby, but he isn't the winner. That distinction belongs to Ted Stepien, who owned the Cleveland Cavaliers in the 1980s. During his disastrous three years, the Cavaliers won 28, 15, and 23 games. He once went through four coaches in one season, only to wind up bringing back the coach he had fired the previous spring. His transactions were so misguid-ed—including trading the first-round pick that the Lakers used for James Worthy in exchange for a career six-points-per-game forward named Don Ford—that the NBA instituted a regulation that teams can't trade first-round picks in consecutive drafts. It's known as the "Ted Stepien Rule."

Sterling never sank to such levels of ineptitude that the league had to enact self-protective measures. And he at least showed savvy business sense when it came to lining his own pockets. Stepien sold the Cavaliers for $20 million in 1983—the year before Magic Johnson and Larry Bird met in the finals and Michael Jordan came into the league, cata-pulting the NBA to a golden era of popularity and profits.

Sterling had bought in just before that, paying $13 million to acquire the Clippers. By 2006, *Forbes* valued the franchise at $285 million. If nothing else, Sterling did get one thing right.

BASEBALL

WHICH DODGER SHOULD BE IN THE HALL OF FAME?

There are two critical questions when it comes to selecting a Hall of Fame player:

1. Did he dominate and/or define his era?
2. Is it possible to tell the history of the game without him?

The gatekeepers to the Cooperstown shrine have already deemed Pee Wee Reese, Duke Snider, Don Sutton, Don Drysdale, Sandy Koufax, Roy Campanella, and Jackie Robinson worthy of admission.

But somehow, 45 years after he became the first player to steal 100 bases, Maury Wills remains outside of the Hall of Fame. To walk through the corridors and not see his bust means visitors aren't getting the complete story.

If you're going to describe the rise of base-running in baseball, the story has to start with Maury Wills. He led the National League in stolen bases for six consecutive seasons at the start of the 1960s, and in the process he helped change the game. He ranks 19th in career stolen bases, with 586.

You think the No. 19 home run hitter (Mel Ott) would get shut out of the Hall of Fame? Not a chance.

The No. 19 RBI man (Reggie Jackson)?

Even the man who ranks 19th in walks (Jimmie Foxx) is in.

The fact is, stolen bases are underappreciated in baseball.

"The guys who hit home runs drive big cars," Wills likes to say.

If baseball is the game that people say it is—thoughtful, strategic, long periods of suspense punctuated by bursts of action—then it should place more value on the assets Wills brought to the table.

The stolen base upped the athletic quotient of the game, just as Babe Ruth's blasts brought power to the sport. If you doubt the importance of a stolen base, just ask the legions of Red Sox fans whose lifetime of misery began to change when Dave Roberts swiped second base in the bottom of the ninth inning of the fourth game of the 2006 American League championship series.

Wills received his due recognition in his breakthrough season of 1962, when he hit .299, scored 130 runs, stole a record-setting 104 bases, and was named MVP.

He received his just rewards when he won three championships with the Dodgers.

But he hasn't received his deserving place among the all-time greats.

The latest snub came from the Veterans Committee in 2007.

It's hard to argue that Wills doesn't meet the criteria for shortstop. Wills might not have been Ozzie Smith in the field, but he did win two Gold Gloves. You can't expect him to be like the large-sized shortstops of recent years, such as Cal Ripken and Alex Rodriguez.

As for his predecessors, Wills had more hits, scored more runs, and, of course, stole more bases than Dave Bancroft, a shortstop from earlier in the 20th century who is in the Hall of Fame.

Sure the game had changed by Wills' era. But he helped change it some more.

Wills paved the way for Lou Brock, who was the forerunner for Rickey Henderson. These were men who could turn a leadoff walk into a game-changing event. All of a sudden, that man on first would become a runner on third, ready to score on a ball put into play.

Wills still serves the Dodgers today, instructing the next generation of ballplayers on how to run the base paths. Even a Juan Pierre, who stole 335 bases before he signed with the Dodgers as a free agent in 2006, stops and listens to what Wills has to say.

They know they're getting lessons from a man who is a part of baseball history...which means he should be a part of the Hall of Fame.

WHICH DODGER SHOULD NOT BE IN THE HALL OF FAME?

Let's review those Hall of Fame criteria again:

1. Did he dominate and/or define his era?
2. Can you tell the history of the game without him?

Now let's ask another question: If you're talking about Don Sutton, is the answer to those questions, "Yes"?

No, no, and no.

He barely even defined the Dodgers in the 1970s, let alone the game of baseball. Yes, he was the Dodgers' opening day starter for seven straight years. But what's more important, the way a season starts, or how it ends? That's important because he wound up leading the Dodgers starters in victories only twice during the decade. And in the defining moments, the 1977 and 1978 World Series games against the New York Yankees, Sutton allowed 34 hits and 17 earned runs in 28 innings.

Of course there's one number that explains Sutton's presence in the Hall of Fame: 324. That's his career victory total, giving him the magic 300 mark that's a sure ticket to Cooperstown.

But those 324 victories were more a tribute to longevity than a sign of greatness. Sutton never won a Cy Young award. He had only one 20-win season (1976, when he went 21–10 with a 3.06 earned run average).

What happened was Sutton started 756 games. Only two members of the 300 club started more: Cy Young (who started 815 games, completed 749 of them, and won 511) and Nolan Ryan (who started 773 games and won the same number as Sutton: 324).

So what makes Ryan a worthier candidate? Those 5,714 strikeouts and seven no-hitters, both records.

You hear Roger Clemens compared to Nolan Ryan as a compliment. Does anyone ever say, "This pitcher reminds me of Don Sutton"? Or, "This kid has a chance to be the next Don Sutton"? Those are the intangibles that should be part of a Hall of Fame resume.

The problem for Sutton is his career is reminiscent of Bert Blyleven's—and Blyleven is not in the Hall of Fame.

Sutton's line: 324 wins, 256 losses, 3.26 ERA, 5,282 ⅓ innings pitched, 4,692 hits, 1,343 walks, and 3,574 strikeouts. He led the National League with nine shutouts in 1972.

Blyleven's line: 287 wins, 250 losses, 3.31 ERA, 4,970 ⅓ innings pitched, 4,632 hits, 1,322 walks, and 3,701 strikeouts. He led the American League in shutouts, with nine in 1973.

Obviously what kept Blyleven locked out was that he couldn't get the 13 more victories to get him to 300. If he had spent most of the 1970s pitching for the Dodgers instead of the Minnesota Twins, he probably would have. Yes, Blyleven allowed more hits and walks per inning pitched, but he also spent all but three seasons of his career in the American League, which meant facing designated hitters instead of the pitchers.

But back to the Dodgers.

When you think of the pitchers in the 1960s, you think of Sandy Koufax and Don Drysdale. In the early 1980s, Fernandomania. In the late 1980s, Orel Hershiser. The 1970s were a mix of Andy Messersmith, Burt Hooton, Tommy John, and, yes, Sutton.

Did you know offhand that he was the franchise's all-time wins leader? He probably wouldn't be your first guess. And that's the problem. A Hall of Famer should be foremost in your thoughts.

Those 233 wins would make him a candidate for a Dodgers Hall of Fame. Their obscurity demean his place in the baseball Hall of Fame.

WHAT WAS THE MOST IMPORTANT DODGERS HOME RUN IN 1988?

We all know every last detail of the most *dramatic* home run. No need to pop in a DVD; you can call up the images and sounds in your mind's screen: Kirk Gibson limping to the plate in the ninth inning of Game 1 of the 1988 World Series, sending a ball to the right-field bleachers, Vin Scully finalizing it with "...she is gone!", Gibson's fist pumping as he rounds second base. Great theater.

But do you know anything about the most important home run in that postseason?

It came in Game 4 of the National League championship series against the New York Mets. The Dodgers trailed the series, two games to one. And they were down, 4–2, in the top of the ninth inning. Mets starter Dwight Gooden was closing in on a complete game, having held the Dodgers to one hit after the first inning.

Gooden walked John Shelby to lead off the ninth inning.

Then it happened. Mike Scioscia hit a home run to right field, and the game was tied.

This was more shocking than Gibson's World Series

home run, even in Gibson's hobbled state. Gibson was the National League MVP that year. He had hit 25 home runs that season, back in the days when that was good enough to rank seventh in the league. For his career, he averaged one home run for every 11 postseason at-bats.

Scioscia hit only three home runs in 408 at-bats in 1988. He had hit one home run in four postseason series prior to this one. But Scioscia happened to be in the hitting groove of his playoff life that particular round. He wound up with eight hits in 22 at-bats in that NLCS, the only playoff series in which he hit over .300.

Scioscia's home run kept the Dodgers alive in that game, setting the stage for Gibson's often-overlooked winning home run in the top of the 12th inning. If Scioscia hadn't hit his home run, Gibson wouldn't have gotten the chance to hit his home run, or the chance to hit the home run everyone remembers.

The Dodgers were three outs away from being down 3–1. They would have had no margin for error and no chance to start Hershiser until Game 7. Gloom and doom.

There wasn't as much riding on Game 1 of the World Series when Gibson hit his famous home run. The Dodgers would start Hershiser in Game 2, as close as it got to a sure thing at that time. He wound up throwing a shutout in that start. He would be available once and possibly twice more during the World Series. And the rest of the Dodgers staff had solved Oakland's supposedly superior lineup: Mark

131

McGwire and Jose Canseco wound up with one hit apiece for the series.

Gibson had only one hit, too: the one that gets replayed again and again, the one that overshadows the home run that mattered the most.

WHAT WAS THE GREATEST TOMMY LASORDA RANT?

42 Over the past 30 years, Tommy Lasorda has become the face of the Dodgers. But sometimes we think of that face getting red and spewing out expletives. That's part of what makes Tommy, Tommy. It's the unbridled emotion.

Another thing that's made him such a fan favorite is his ability to laugh at himself. He even willingly subjected himself to a chorus of boos when he took one last walk across the field at Candlestick Park when the Dodgers played their final game there before the Giants moved to downtown San Francisco. And who can forget the expression on his face after the shards of Vladimir Guerrero's broken bat caused him to tumble backward in the 2001 All-Star Game in Seattle?

So what was the quintessential Tommy moment? Let's count down through the nominees.

4. EATING RAU

When the New York Yankees got three straight hits off Doug Rau in the third inning of Game 4 in the 1977 World

Series, Lasorda had seen enough. He went to the mound to get Rau out of there. A microphone Lasorda was wearing captured this exchange:

Rau: I feel good, Tommy.

Lasorda: I don' give a [bleep] you feel good. There's four mother[bleepin'] hits up there.

Rau: They're all the opposite way.

Lasorda: I don't give a [bleep].

Rau: They've got a left-handed hitter. I can strike this mother[bleeper] out.

Lasorda: I don't give a [bleep], Dougie. I might be wrong, but that's my [bleepin'] job. I'll make the [bleepin'] decisions here. Keep your [bleepin'] mouth shut!

3. ON BOATS AND BEVACQUA

San Diego Padres infielder Kurt Bevacqua's crack on Lasorda prompted this outburst:

"[Bleeping] Bevacqua, who couldn't hit water if he fell out a [bleeping] boat...."

And:

"I guaran-[bleeping]-tee you this, when I pitched and I was gonna pitch against a [bleeping] team that had guys on it like Bevacqua, I'd send a [bleeping] limousine to get the [bleeper] to make sure he was in the mother[bleeping] lineup because I'd kick that [bleeper's] ass any [bleeping] day of the week. He's a [bleeping] mother[bleeping] big-mouth, I'll tell you that."

2. KING COMMENT

After Chicago Cubs outfielder Dave Kingman hit three home runs against the Dodgers, a reporter asked Lasorda, "What's your opinion of Kingman's performance?" An innocent question led to an all-time tirade:

"What's my opinion of Kingman's performance!? What the [bleep] do you think is my opinion of it? I think it was [bleeping bleep]. Put that in, I don't [bleep]. Opinion of his performance!!? [Bleep], he beat us with three [bleeping] home runs! What the [bleep] do you mean, 'What is my opinion of his performance?' How could you ask me a question like that, 'What is my opinion of his performance?' [Bleep], he hit three home runs! [Bleep]. I'm [bleeping] pissed off to lose that [bleeping] game. And you ask me my opinion of his performance! [Bleep.] That's a tough question to ask me, isn't it? 'What is my opinion of his performance?'"

1. OROSCO'S ORDERS

As classic as those rants were, they didn't accomplish anything other than to give longtime L.A. radio host Jim Healy some go-to material over the years.

But during Game 4 of the 1988 National League championship series against the Mets, Lasorda had a quintessential Tommy moment. It was animated, it was profane—and more important, it got results. There's no audio recording, but anyone reading lips could get the message.

The Dodgers were up by a run in the bottom of the 12th

inning. With one out, runners on first and second, and left-handed hitters Keith Hernandez and Darryl Strawberry due up, the left-handed Jesse Orosco walked Hernandez to load the bases. Lasorda came out to the mound to both talk some sense into Orosco and give Orel Hershiser more time to warm up in the bullpen. (Yes, he was about to use Hershiser in relief. Another classic case of Lasorda squeezing everything he could out of his top pitchers.) After a shaky performance from Orosco in the previous game, Lasorda had asked God to strike him down if he ever used Orosco again. But he was out of pitchers in this extra-inning game, forcing him to go with the aging veteran and to tell the Man upstairs: "I was just kidding."

On the mound, Lasorda took out his frustration on Orosco. "I'm tired of looking at your [bleep]!" Lasorda screamed. Then he issued a demand: "Throw a [bleeping] strike!" What it lacked in word count, it made up for in impact.

Orosco got Strawberry to pop up. Then Hershiser came in and got Kevin McReynolds to fly to center. Game over. Mission accomplished. No Tommy rant, and it's possible Strawberry would have gotten a game-winning hit and the Mets would have won the pivotal game and the series. Instead, the Dodgers went on to win the championship.

At a party after the playoffs were over, Orosco told Lasorda he had never been spoken to the way Lasorda talked to him on the mound that night.

Lasorda replied: "It worked, didn't it?"

WHO ARE THE ALL-TIME BEST L.A. DODGERS?

CATCHER: MIKE PIAZZA

An easy call for Los Angeles, and would make for an interesting debate for the all-time Dodgers catcher if pitted against Roy Campanella. There's no shortage of worthy candidates from the Los Angeles days alone. John Roseboro, Mike Scioscia, and Steve Yeager all logged more than 1,200 games behind the plate for the Dodgers. Scioscia was a master of blocking the plate, and Yeager hit 100 home runs.

But Piazza is one of the greatest-hitting catchers of all time, the all-time leader for home runs at the position, and his best years came with the Dodgers, where he was the Rookie of the Year, a six-time All-Star and twice the MVP runner-up. Piazza batted .331 with 177 home runs and 585 RBI as a Dodger. His best year was 1997, when he hit .362, bashed 40 home runs, and drove in 124—all career highs.

FIRST BASE: STEVE GARVEY

Eric Karros hit more home runs than any Dodger since the franchise moved to Los

Angeles, but Garvey was a 10-time All-Star and the 1974 National League MVP, not to mention a four-time Gold Glove winner who played in 1,207 consecutive games.

While Karros was a consistent producer—at one point passing the 30-home run, 100-RBI mark in five out of six seasons—Garvey maintained a spot among the elite for most of his Dodgers days. He ranked among the National League's top 10 in batting average six times, in the top 10 in hits nine times, and in the top 10 in home runs seven times.

Plus, he set the standard for perfect hair.

SECOND BASE: DAVEY LOPES

An important part of playing second base is throwing the ball to first base. Sounds ridiculously simple, but Steve Sax's inability to do that basic task for a stretch that included 30 errors in 1983 cost him a shot at this honor.

He was a better batter, with a .280 average in his Dodgers career, surpassing Lopes' .262. And Sax was pretty speedy, swiping 290 bases with the Dodgers.

Lopes was better in the field and had more power. He won a Gold Glove in 1978 and, more surprisingly, finished eighth in the National League in home runs the next year, with 28. He spent most of his career running the base-paths at full speed, not in a home run trot, and finished second only to Maury Wills among Dodgers stolen base leaders.

SHORTSTOP: MAURY WILLS

The only all-time infielder who didn't play in the block that came up together in the 1970s, Wills did his damage a decade earlier. During his first stint with the Dodgers from 1959–66, he created a new place in the game for people such as Lopes. Wills was the first to break the 100-steal mark in a season and set a Dodgers franchise record with 490.

Wills' final years with the Dodgers overlapped with the runner-up at this position, Bill Russell. Russell spent his entire 18-year career with the Dodgers, logging 1,746 games at shortstop. He made three All-Star teams and ranks among the franchise's top 10 in hits and doubles.

Bill Russell was steady, but Wills was revolutionary.

THIRD BASE: RON CEY

"The Penguin" ranks among the L.A. Dodgers, top 10 in hits, home runs, doubles, RBI, and runs. And we're still wondering how he survived that Goose Gossage fastball to the dome in the 1981 World Series.

Adrian Beltre had a chance to take over this position. He could have locked it up for a decade and surpassed all of Cey's numbers. He came up to the big-league club during the tumultuous summer of 1998, one of Tommy Lasorda's first moves after becoming the interim general manager. Beltre often disappointed, but would put together enough of a season to post typical numbers of 20 home runs and 80

RBI. In 2004 he finally had a complete year, batting .334, with 48 home runs and 121 RBI...then he left for Seattle as a free agent. He didn't come close to matching those numbers again, just as he never lived up to his potential to become the Dodgers' greatest third baseman.

RIGHT FIELD: SHAWN GREEN

Raul Mondesi was the most talented player to patrol this patch of Dodger Stadium, but his career wasn't allowed to flourish in L.A. He booked himself an early flight out of town when, after getting benched for being late to a game, he went on a tirade to the media that peaked with "[Bleep] Davey and [bleep] Malone." That would be manager Davey Johnson and general manager Kevin Malone, and that was the beginning of the end.

In only five years with the Dodgers, Shawn Green hit 164 home runs (one more than Mondesi), and was much less controversial. He also managed to hit three playoff home runs to Mondesi's zero, despite half as many playoff at-bats as Mondesi.

CENTER FIELD: WILLIE DAVIS

The speedy outfielder helped symbolize the changing game and the new era of the Dodgers in the 1960s. Davis took over the center field spot from legendary Brooklyn Dodger Duke Snider, and he is the L.A. Dodgers' all-time hits leader (2,091), winning three Gold Gloves. Although he didn't record as many stolen bases as Maury Wills, on offense he used his speed to lead the league in triples twice. On defense, Davis' fleet feet enabled him to get to so many balls, he finished his career in the all-time top 10 in putouts. Davis had a 31-game hitting streak that stands as the longest in Dodgers history. He also had a moment of infamy in Game 2 of the 1966 World Series, when he recorded three errors on two consecutive plays.

Davis was traded to Montreal in 1973. Honorable mention here goes to Rick Monday, who came along in the 1970s. While Monday's power numbers never matched his peak years with the Chicago Cubs, he did provide two memorable moments in Dodgers history: the time he snatched an American flag from two fans who ran on the field and attempted to set Old Glory on fire, and his home run to beat the Montreal Expos in Game 5 of the 1981 World Series.

LEFT FIELD: GARY SHEFFIELD

Like Mondesi, Gary Sheffield was another great hitter whose mouth shortened his Dodgers career. Sheffield arrived as part of the infamous Mike Piazza trade in 1998, and fans were too busy mourning the popular Piazza's departure to notice the numbers Sheffield put up. His .312 batting average as a Dodger was third in L.A. history (Piazza, alas, was first, at .331). He also managed to creep into the L.A. Dodgers, top 15 in home runs in only 3 ½ seasons in Dodgers Blue, hitting 129 (including 43 in the 2000 season). Sheffield, who seemingly always wanted more money, had a beef with team CEO Bob Daly, and it got him traded to Atlanta in 2002.

Dusty Baker had more than twice as many Dodgers at-bats as Sheffield, but hit only five more home runs during his eight seasons in Los Angeles. Baker arrived in 1976, was a two-time All-Star, and played on three World Series teams. Now he's probably thought of more as the former manager of the San Francisco Giants than a former outfielder for the Dodgers. He was a part of a nostalgic era for the Dodgers, but he never was as feared at the plate as Sheffield.

LEFT-HANDED STARTING PITCHER: SANDY KOUFAX

Dodger Stadium is a pitchers' ballpark. You see it in the box score, you see it when fly balls die in the cool night air, and you definitely see it when looking through the team history book. Most of the franchise's greatest hitters played most or all of their careers in Brooklyn, while most of the great pitchers played in Los Angeles.

And the top two pitchers in victories (Don Sutton and Don Drysdale) and five of the top six in strikeouts (Sutton, Drysdale, Koufax, Fernando Valenzuela, and Orel Hershiser) are L.A. guys.

Who's No. 1? Among lefties, there's no question: It's

Koufax. He's the definitive Dodgers pitcher, shrouded in a Dimaggio-like mystique. Few pitchers could have a missed start add to their legend, but Koufax's decision to sit out Game 1 of the 1965 World Series because it fell on the Jewish holy day of Yom Kippur earned him respect for abiding by his principles and only added to the Koufax lore.

Then there's the production. The four no-hitters, including the perfect game. The final four years of his career, which went like this: 25–5, 1.88 ERA, and 306 strikeouts in 1963; 19–5, 1.74 ERA, and 223 strikeouts in 1964, 26–8, 2.04 ERA, and 382 strikeouts in 1965, and 27–9, 1.73 ERA, and 317 strikeouts in 1966. During that span he won the Cy Young award three times and the National League MVP.

The biggest flaw with Koufax's career is that it ended too soon, due to arthritis and arm complications that led him to retire at age 30. But that four-year stretch of unparalleled excellence is enough to give Koufax the edge over Valenzuela.

Valenzuela's career was the opposite of Koufax's, who had a losing record after his first four seasons. After Valenzuela's Big Bang rookie year that saw him haul in a Cy Young Award and a World Series championship, Valenzuela came back with a 19–13, 2.87 ERA, 199-strikeout year in 1982 and set career highs with 21 victories and 242 strikeouts in 1986. He threw a no-hitter in 1990, in what turned out to be his last season with the Dodgers. Valenzuela logged an average of 269 innings per season

143

from 1982–86, and the strain all of those screwballs put on his left arm turned him into an ordinary pitcher after that. He had a record of 42–48 from 1987–90 and was released in the spring of 1991. It left him short of Koufax on the franchise wins list (141 to Koufax's 165) and his ERA elevated beyond Koufax range (3.31 to Koufax's 2.76). Don't take it as a knock that Valenzuela couldn't measure up to Koufax. Neither could any other left-hander in baseball history.

RIGHT-HANDED STARTING PITCHER: DON DRYSDALE

Did we ever get a definitive answer on what the "D" in "Big D" stands for? Is it Don, or Drysdale? Or Dominant? Or maybe it's short for Dodgers' Best Right-handed Pitcher of all Time, because that title belongs to Drysdale.

Orel Hershiser might have surpassed Drysdale's run of 58 consecutive scoreless innings, and Drysdale didn't come as close to single-handedly delivering a championship the way Hershiser did with his three wins, one save, and 1.06 in the 1988 postseason.

But in the pitching-heavy decade of the 1960s, Drysdale was one of the best to take the mound. His best season was the Cy Young-winning campaign of 1962, when he led the National League in wins (25) and strikeouts (232). But he finished among the league's top three strikeout leaders four other times during the 1960s.

Another notable statistic: He finished among the league's

top five in hit batters every year from 1960 to 1968. It wasn't because he lacked control; he consistently ranked among the fewest walks allowed per nine innings. When he hit someone he was sending a message, claiming ownership of home plate and the inside part of the batter's box as well.

Perhaps his meanness was just a by-product of his toughness. He lasted until the final out 167 times, a finish-the-job mentality that was unmatched in the Los Angeles Dodgers annals. Don Sutton won more games than Drysdale's 209 and Sandy Koufax had a lower ERA than his 2.95, but no one ever had more determination. Perhaps that's what the D stood for.

RELIEF PITCHER: ERIC GAGNE

Eric Gagne is the Dodgers' all-time saves leader with 167, mostly based on three outstanding years. In the middle of that stretch—2003—he converted all 55 of his save opportunities and won the NL Cy Young award. He also set a record by converting 84 consecutive save opportunities.

Gagne became the most popular athlete in Los Angeles during that stretch. His ninth-inning entrances became an event, with "Game Over" flashing on the scoreboard as "Welcome to the Jungle" blared over the loudspeakers.

Sure, he came along in the era of specialization and didn't have to work as hard as say, Mike Marshall, a "closer" who averaged two innings per appearance.

Marshall appeared in 106 games in 1974, the first of his two years with the Dodgers. Marshall won the Cy Young award by winning 15 games and saving 21 others.

Gagne only averaged one inning as a reliever, but that was often all he needed to do his job.

MANAGER: TOMMY LASORDA

The narrowest field of any Dodgers debate: It's either Lasorda or Walter Alston. They were the only Dodgers managers the first 40 years the team was in L.A. Both are in the Hall of Fame. They were complete contrasts in styles, with Alston maintaining a cool demeanor and Lasorda liable to fly into a rage, whether in an argument with an umpire or at a postgame meeting with reporters.

Alston's teams went to five World Series and won three. Lasorda's went to four World Series and won two. Alston won Manager of the Year six times, Lasorda won it twice. So why does Lasorda get the nod? Because this was his victorious lineup in Game 4 of the 1988 World Series: Steve Sax, Franklin Stubbs, Mickey Hatcher, Mike Davis, John Shelby, Mike Scioscia, Danny Heep, Jeff Hamilton, and Alfredo Griffin. NBC's Bob Costas was right when he said it was the weakest-hitting lineup in World Series history. And Lasorda was savvy enough to use Costas' words as a rallying cry for his team, leading them to a championship they had no business winning against a loaded Oakland team that featured Jose Canseco and Mark McGwire.

WAS CORPORATE OWNERSHIP THAT BAD FOR THE DODGERS AND ANGELS?

Southern California sports fans were still adjusting to Disney's takeover of the Angels when the unthinkable news came out in January of 1997: Peter O'Malley was selling the Dodgers.

The Dodgers had been run by Peter and his father, Walter, for more than half a century. Peter, stung by the city's refusal to back his bid to build a football stadium and put an NFL team in Chavez Ravine, decided that trying to run a baseball team as a family business no longer made sense. O'Malley worried about his ability to keep pace with the escalating salaries. And with an aging stadium that lacked premium seats and luxury boxes, the Dodgers did not have the same means to generate revenues as other teams.

The Angels had already felt the squeeze of baseball's broken business model and were piling up debt when they considered selling in 1990. Owners Gene and Jackie Autry actually sought out Disney, going to CEO Michael Eisner's office in Burbank to sell the idea. He turned them down initially, but five years later, encouraged by the initial success of Disney's Mighty Ducks NHL franchise, agreed to buy the team and take over the Autrys' debt.

Meanwhile, Fox quickly emerged as the leading buyer for the Dodgers after the "For Sale" sign went up. In many ways, the thought process was the same as Disney's: programming. Disney, which also owned ESPN, planned to make the Angels the anchor of a proposed "ESPN West" regional sports channel, and hoped to lure the Dodgers as well. But Fox had its own regional network to look after, and owning the Dodgers could be a cornerstone of the programming package.

Fox's "Fox Sports West" (which later changed to the generic Fox Sports Net, then simply FSN) won out, and ESPN West never launched.

But neither corporate giant stayed in the ball game for too long. Baseball's economics were just too dysfunctional to justify the annual losses to the shareholders. Disney handed the Angels over to Arturo Moreno in 2003 after seven years of ownership, and Frank McCourt took the Dodgers from Fox in 2004, only six years after Fox bought the team.

The fans said good riddance to the corporations. They ridiculed Disney's ill-advised attempts to add cheerleaders to baseball games and they winced at the cartoonish uniforms that featured—in what had to be a first for the sport—the color periwinkle. Many always thought the

Angels were too concerned with the bottom line to spend the money necessary to put a winning product on the field.

The Fox era with the Dodgers was recalled for introducing tumult and turnover to a franchise that had known nothing but stability. The Dodgers had two managers from 1954 to 1996. Under Fox, the Dodgers had four in the course of four years. They also went through five general managers during their regime. But most egregious was the Fox suits trading fan favorite Mike Piazza to the Florida Marlins while keeping the general manager out of the loop.

Those were emotional reactions to the side effects of doing business. If we can take the team caps off and put on an accountant's glasses, it's clear that the Dodgers and Angels were better off in the long run for having corporate ownership in the 1990s.

The Angels might have left Anaheim. They had a bad lease situation and had no means to make Anaheim Stadium work. But after Disney took over, the Mouse House spent most of the $118 million it cost to convert Anaheim Stadium back to a baseball-only ballpark, and gave it a charm it never had before. And while Disney didn't spend big on free agents (with the notable exception of the ill-fated $80 million splurge on Mo Vaughn), it allowed the Angels to keep the core of homegrown players that wound up winning the World Series in 2002.

Fox never had a problem spending money, it just wasn't spent well. They authorized an industry-changing $105 million contract for Kevin Brown, a pitcher who had never won a Cy Young award and didn't get close to one with the Dodgers. They approved $55 million for Darren Dreifort and $15 million for Carlos Perez.

But they spent money to upgrade Dodger Stadium, adding luxury suites and a stadium club with premium seats behind the dugout.

And as it turned out, the Piazza trade wasn't that devastating. It's not as if the Florida Marlins wound up with the better of the deal; they turned around and dealt Piazza to the New York Mets for three prospects, two of whom you've never heard of.

Gary Sheffield, the best of the players the Dodgers received in the Piazza trade, had several productive years. Even in Piazza's best year with the Mets, when he hit .303 with 40 home runs and 124 RBI, Sheffield came pretty close: .301, 34, and 101.

And by 2001, Paul Lo Duca had taken over the catcher position and won the hearts of Dodgers fans.

In 2004, both the Dodgers and the Angels made the playoffs. It doesn't sound like Disney or Fox did irreparable damage.

WHAT WAS THE WORST ANGELS CHOKE JOB?

This was going to look at the worst chokes by Los Angeles area teams, but it's clear the Angels need this category to themselves. No other local team has put together a compilation of choke jobs as dramatic or even tragic as the Angels.

3. TROUBLE BREWING

Behind complete games from Tommy John and Bruce Kison, the Angels kept the league's most potent offense in check and took the first two games of the 1982 American League championship series from the Brewers at Anaheim Stadium. Since the start of divisional play, no team had blown a 2–0 lead in the best-of-five league championship series. The Brewers took Game 3 back home in Milwaukee. Then Angels manager Gene Mauch decided to bring John back on three days' rest. John lasted only 3⅓ innings, during which he allowed six runs. For Game 5, Mauch brought Kison back on three days' rest—and a still-healing finger that had blistered during Game 2. Kison fought gamely, but Cecil Cooper hit a two-out, two-strike single off reliever Luis Sanchez to give the Brewers a 4–3 victory and a trip to the World Series. The mitigating factors: all three of the losses came in Milwaukee, and the 1982 Angels were prone to losing streaks, having strings of seven and eight losses during the course of the regular season. This three-game streak just happened to come at the worst possible time, in October, when reputations are defined.

2. THE COLLAPSE

Thirteen years (what an unfortunate number) after the Angels made playoff history, they made regular-season history by blowing a double-digit advantage in the standings in record time. In 1995 they held an 11-game lead in the American League West division on August 9. They were 10 ½ games ahead on August 16 and were caught by the Seattle Mariners on September 20, the fastest a lead that size had disappeared in the 20th century, the Elias Sports Bureau reported. The Angels were done in by a pair of nine-game losing streaks, an injury to shortstop Gary DiSarcina, and the inability of staff ace Chuck Finley to win a game for more than a month. A five-game winning streak at the end of the season only served to prolong the agony, forcing a one-game playoff in Seattle that the Mariners won behind Randy Johnson.

1. THE PITCH

It's one thing to blow leads and lose playoff games on the road. True agony is to be at home, with police ready to keep celebratory fans off the field, champagne chilling, needing only one strike to send the franchise to its first World Series…and watching it all vanish in the time it takes for a ball to disappear over the left center field wall.

In their first trip to the postseason since the Milwaukee series, the Angels were finally able to get to three wins first. But by 1986 the ALCS was a best-of-seven series. Still, the Angels won three of the first four games and were ahead, 5–2, in the bottom of the ninth inning. Starting pitcher Mike Witt was closing in on a complete game when Don Baylor, the designated hitter the Angels let go after the 1982 season, hit a two-run home run for Boston. Witt didn't get to finish. Gene Mauch brought in Gary Lucas, who hit Rich Gedman with his first pitch, and then Mauch summoned Donnie Moore to face Dave Henderson.

With two strikes, Henderson hit a home run to give the Red Sox a 6–5 lead.

In the years that followed, people forgot the fact that the Angels tied the score in the bottom of the ninth and had the winning run at third base with one out and couldn't get him home. They'd have a hard time remembering that Henderson's actual game-winning RBI came on a sacrifice fly in the 11th inning. And they forget that the Angels still had two more chances to win the series when they went to Boston for Games 6 and 7.

Everything changed with that Donnie Moore pitch, a split-fingered fastball that didn't drop low enough. Nothing else that transpired—including Bill Buckner's inability to scoop up a simple ground ball in Game 6 of the World Series–happened without that pitch. And we'll always wonder about the role that fateful pitch had in Moore's decision to end his life in 1989.

We do know the Angels never got as good a chance to give a World Series trip to their owner, Gene Autry.

It's all enough to make a person get all (ahem) choked up.

SERIOUSLY, THE LOS ANGELES ANGELS OF ANAHEIM?

 In 2005, the Angels made baseball history when they changed cities without actually moving.

Ignoring geography and the wishes of its most loyal fans, owner Arturo Moreno switched his team's name from the Anaheim Angels to the Los Angeles Angels of Anaheim.

They tacked on the "of Anaheim" part to satisfy language in the contract the previous owner, the Walt Disney Company, had with the city. As it turned out, it did more to provide comedians with material than it did to keep the city happy.

The extreme example came when a Long Beach minor league team announced it was renaming itself the Long Beach Armada of Los Angeles of California of the United States of North America Including Barrow, Alaska.

But for all the jokes, all the mocking and the ridicule, it was a good idea. The team is more valuable and profitable than ever, and the locals didn't turn their backs on the Angels.

Moreno's rationale was: Why restrict the branding of his team to a city of 300,000 when he could tap into a broader population of 16 million? When the Angels changed their name, they revealed that only 360 of their season-ticket accounts (representing 1,104 seats, or 5 percent of the stock) belonged to people who had an Anaheim address.

One component of the name change was to broaden the ticket-buying pool. The Angels launched a billboard campaign that put 480 signs reading "City of Angels" (with the team's signature halo topping the A) in locales stretching from Bellflower to Encino to Santa Monica.

But this was really about attracting sponsors.

Los Angeles is a concept as much as it is an actual physical place. Because of the unique, sprawling nature of the city, millions of people say they're from Los Angeles, without actually living in Los Angeles. Moreover, people around the country and around the world associate various parts of Southern California with Los Angeles. People think of Disneyland in the context of Los Angeles, and it's right down Katella from Angel Stadium.

Local fans responded with a couple of billboards of their own, protesting the name. Many people live in Orange County specifically because it *isn't* Los Angeles, and they're fiercely protective of their separate identities.

The real fight came from the city of Anaheim, which claimed the Angels violated their contract and spent millions of dollars fighting them in court. The Angels won a jury decision, and they went on using the Los Angeles Angels of Anaheim moniker.

Fully aware that most of the fans at home games are from Orange County, the Angels consciously try to avoid insulting or antagonizing them. You don't see the words Los Angeles around Angel Stadium. When they take the field, they are announced as "Your Angels."

But again, it's not about what happens in that stadium. It's about the broader world, and that's where Moreno had his desired effect.

The new television contract the Angels signed with the local Fox sports network was worth up to $500 million. Big-time national sponsors include General Motors, Pepsi, Anheuser-Busch, and Bank of America. Since 2005, annual revenues went from $147 million to $187 million, and the value of the franchise went from $294 million to $431 million.

Make all the jokes you want. Arturo Moreno once sold his Outdoor Advertising company for $8.3 billion. He probably knows more about marketing than you.

WHO ARE THE ALL-TIME BEST ANGELS?

DESIGNATED HITTER: DON BAYLOR

In many ways, Baylor was the prototypical designated hitter, and he certainly set the standard for the Angels. Big Don was the American League MVP in 1979, when he batted .296 with 36 home runs and a league-leading 139 RBI. It was one of the rare times when the Angels manned the position with a star player in the prime of his career. Actually, he played the majority of that season in the outfield. But Baylor was a designated hitter for all but six of his games in his final two years with the Angels. And he spent so much time at DH in the final six years of his career after he left the Angels in 1982 that it's hard to remember him with a glove.

Reggie Jackson was another slugger who played more outfield than designated hitter after he came to the Angels. But he did his best hitting, ironically, as an outfielder with his 39-home run season in 1982.

After Jackson, the position steadily decreased in value for the Angels. There was Brian Downing at the end of his career. They got a few solid years out of Chili Davis before the position became almost an afterthought for them.

It's hard to believe the Angels won a World Series with

Brad Fullmer (19 home runs, 59 RBI) at DH. Then again, they did play more of a National League style of ball under Manager Mike Scioscia. Maybe they forget that in the American League you can have a big, immobile guy who does nothing but bash the ball.

CATCHER: BOB BOONE

If nothing else, Boone deserves credit for logging almost 1,000 games for the Angels at the sport's most grueling position. But Boone wasn't just a backstop; he won three Gold Glove awards and swung the bat well enough to rank in the franchise's top 20 for hits. This spot might have belonged to Brian Downing if he stayed at the catcher position.

Downing played behind the plate for most of his first two seasons after he got to the Angels in 1978. But after he hit the weight room and switched to that distinctive batting stance (with the front leg turned halfway back to the dugout), his bat became so valuable that the Angels didn't want to risk him getting injured catching balls and blocking home. He had his best seasons after moving to the outfield.

Todd Greene showed some potential as a power hitter in the minor leagues (.290 average with 9 home runs in 124 at-bats in 1997). But in one of those injuries that only seemed to happen to the Angels, he broke his hand in batting practice and never seemed the same afterward.

FIRST BASE: ROD CAREW

Perhaps if Wally Joyner hadn't left as a free agent after the 1991 season, when he was 29 years old, he would have earned this spot. Our pick here also spent his peak years elsewhere, but he managed to make a bigger impact when he was with the Angels. Rod Carew won seven batting titles in Minnesota. Still, he was an All-Star in all but the last of his seven seasons with the Angels. He also picked up his 3,000th hit while wearing an Angels uniform. While Carew never had a season as exciting as Wally Joyner's "Wally World" days of 1987, when Joyner hit 34 home runs, Carew still finished with seven more hits than Joyner as an Angel, despite almost 300 fewer at-bats.

SECOND BASE: BOBBY GRICH

In many ways, Grich was the quintessential Angel: a good fielder, and a decent hitter with decent power. One of those guys who, when you look back on it, makes you say, "He did what?" In Grich's case, the surprise stat is that he led the American League in home runs during the strike-shortened 1981 season. And when you tallied up the numbers from Grich's 10-year Angels career that ended in 1986, he was sixth on the franchise's all-time hits list (1,103), sixth in home runs (154), and sixth in RBI (557).

Adam Kennedy might have pulled a little closer if he

stayed longer in Anaheim. Still, Kennedy gave the Angels a credible hitter at the bottom of the lineup during the seven years after his arrival in 2000.

And if Howie Kendrick reaches his potential and enjoys a lengthy career with the Angels, this spot will probably belong to him one day.

SHORTSTOP: JIM FREGOSI

It's not often that an Angel could be considered the dominant player at his position for a decade, but that's a fitting description for Fregosi in the 1960s. He was a six-time All-Star. Since then, the Angels shortstops have mostly been overachievers such as Dick Schofield and David Eckstein. Fregosi gets this spot easily.

If this were a popularity contest it would go to Eckstein, the little shortstop that could. He's so beloved in Orange County that even after he left the Angels to join the Cardinals, a book signing he held at the Richard Nixon Presidential Library in Yorba Linda drew hundreds of fans who waited for hours in a line that doubled back across the replica West Wing and down the hall to the main lobby.

Fregosi has the temperament of a wet elephant. But it's the numbers, not his personality, that win out here: 1,408 hits (fifth in franchise history), 691 runs (fifth), 546 RBI (seventh), and six All-Star appearances.

THIRD BASE: TROY GLAUS

Doug DeCinces held this spot for years, and is good enough to rank among the franchise's top 15 in the major hitting categories. But Troy Glaus did more in less time, and the way he destroyed the ball during the 2002 World Series puts him over the top. The Angels let him escape as a free agent, thinking they could replace him more cheaply with Dallas McPherson. It's one of the more boneheaded decisions in Angels history.

Yes, the Angels found themselves wondering about the true severity of his injuries when Glaus missed games (he played in only 149 games over his last two seasons in Anaheim). They also weren't happy with his propensity to whiff; he struck out 1,360 times with them. But he pounded the ball when he was in the lineup and made contact with the ball, and during his seven seasons with the Angels he cranked out 182 home runs in 2,962 at-bats. He's also the only member of the Angels' top 10 RBI leaders with fewer than 3,000 at-bats.

RIGHT FIELD: VLADIMIR GUERRERO

It's hard to go against Tim Salmon, Mr. Angel, the man who wore the broadest smile when the Angels won it all in 2002. It's hard to go against the franchise home run leader. He stood in right field for more than a decade, including one lonely season when the right field seats were deserted while the stadium underwent renovations. But it won't look good if someone picks up this book a few years from now and doesn't see Guerrero's name here. He was the American League MVP in 2004, his first season with the Angels, when he hit .337 with 39 home runs and 126, and single-handedly carried the team to the AL West pennant down the stretch. After only four seasons with the Angels, he was already creeping up on the franchise's top 10 lists. He is easily the best free-agent signing in the team's history.

CENTER FIELD: JIM EDMONDS

Fred Lynn was one of the Angels' early high-profile free agents when he came to California from the Boston Red Sox in 1981. He made the All-Star Game three times, but had a tougher time making the field for the regular-season games; he played in as many as 140 games only once during his four years with the Angels. Jim Edmonds was cut from the same cloth: capable of making spectacular catches, but also prone to injuries. Edmonds played in more than 133 games only twice during his six full seasons with the big-league club. When he did play, Edmonds was capable of putting up 33 homers and 107 RBI, as he did in his All-Star season of 1995. But even when he made it onto the field, the Angels weren't always happy with his play. They even made some behind-the-scenes accusations that Edmonds was prone to taking at-bats off during games; Edmonds was so incensed by that, he made an angry phone call to the beat reporter who wrote the story. He seemed to carry that anger with him after the Angels traded him to St. Louis in 2000. Even though he was entering his 30s, his numbers with the Cardinals were better than his Angels numbers, including a 2004 season in which he put up career highs with 42 RBI and 11 RBI at age 34.

LEFT FIELD: GARRET ANDERSON

Sometimes just showing up is enough. In a franchise that seemed to be perpetually defined by untimely injuries, Anderson played in at least 156 games per year for six consecutive seasons. He drove in at least 116 runs in four of those seasons, and led the league in doubles in 2002 and 2003. Anderson even finished with more home runs than the one-time franchise homer leader and top left field candidate, Brian Downing.

For Downing's consistency (he had a run of at least 20 home runs in six out of seven seasons), the only time he ever led the league in any category was when he walked 106 times in 1987. The fact that his 222 home runs once stood as the franchise record said more about the Angels than about him. It's hard to believe the Angels never had a player hit 300 homers during his time with the team (Salmon topped out at 299).

RIGHT-HANDED STARTING PITCHER: NOLAN RYAN

It's hard to imagine in this day of precise pitch counts, but Ryan completed more than half of the 288 games he started for the Angels from 1972–79. Forty of those games were shutouts. And, of course, major league baseball's all-time strikeout leader is the Angels' K King, with 2,416 strikeouts in 2,181 innings. Also, Ryan threw four of his seven no-hitters with the Angels.

What makes Ryan resonate with us isn't just that he was a power pitcher—he remained a power pitcher. It wasn't as if he had a brief run of glory, then faded away. After the Angels inexplicably let him walk away following his 16–14, 3.60 ERA, 223-strikeout season in 1979, he went on to exceed that strikeout total five times over the 13 years with the Houston Astros and Texas Rangers. In contrast, Frank Tanana, Ryan's Angels contemporary in the 1970s, went from a hard-throwing strikeout threat to a junk-baller who couldn't put a dent in a pillow with the slop he threw toward the plate in his later days with the Detroit Tigers.

The closest right-hander to Ryan on the Angels list is Mike Witt. He had one thing over Ryan—the perfect game he threw on the last day of the 1984 season. But Witt only had three seasons in which he truly pitched like a staff ace, with an ERA under 4.00: from 1984–86, when his record was a combined 48–30.

68 LEFT-HANDED STARTING PITCHER: CHUCK FINLEY

How many teams have more candidates for best left-handed pitcher than best righty? With the Angels, it's a little more crowded on that side of the mound. There's Frank Tanana, with his 102 victories and complete games in nearly half of his 218 starts. There's Mark Langston, who had as fine a season as any Angel when he went 19–8 with a 3.00 ERA in 1991.

But the nod has to go to Chuck Finley. It's not just the team-record 165 wins, combined with 2,151 strikeouts that are second only to Nolan Ryan. It's the way he loved representing the franchise, with just the right attitude to keep baseball in its proper place, making the locker room a fun place. Finley's most quoted line came after he was named American League Player of the Week. "That just shows you how this league has gone to hell," he said.

There's nothing wrong with giving such a good pitcher and good guy his due, so no trepidation here about giving Finley the nod.

69 RELIEVER: TROY PERCIVAL

The 2002 World Series stood as a compact referendum on the hierarchy of the Angels' relief pitchers. Francisco Rodriguez was the exciting young rookie with the electric stuff. But in the end Troy Percival was the king of the hill, securing the final out of Game 7.

Percival is still the all-time reigning reliever as well; his 316 are about twice as many saves as Rodriguez. Rodriguez has the wicked slider in addition to the fastball that seems shot out of a cannon, which was Percival's main weapon.

Will Rodriguez prove to be better? The early numbers are tracking in his favor. He has a better strikeout-to-walk ratio going for him, and he picked up his 100th save at age 24, while Percival got his at age 28.

This is the one ranking most likely to change. But for now, it's Percival's. Besides, he was classy when Rodriguez first came up and it was obvious the kid was about to take his job. Percival ought to get some kind of reward for that.

 ## MANAGER: MIKE SCIOSCIA

The first Angel to win the Manager of the Year award was Bill Rigney, who picked up the hardware in 1962. But Mike Scioscia topped his 2002 Manager of the Year award with a World Series title. So there. And in 2007 Scioscia passed Rigney's franchise record of 625 managerial victories. Scioscia's game-by-game approach sunk in with his players, who never seemed too elated when things went well or too stressed when things went wrong.

COLLEGES

WHAT WAS THE BEST USC–UCLA FOOTBALL GAME?

This is the most subjective argument of them all. One fan's sentimental memory will be part of another fan's painful past that still pops up in therapy sessions. It all depends on whether your replica jersey is blue or cardinal.

For fireworks and excitement, it's hard to top the 1990 game.

Bruins quarterback Tommy Maddox set a school record with 409 passing yards and three touchdowns. USC counterpart Todd Marinovich's numbers weren't as impressive—215 yards and two touchdowns. But Marinovich connected with Johnnie Morton on a touchdown pass with 16 seconds remaining to give USC the 45–42 victory.

At the time, it was the highest-scoring game in the history of the series. But six years later came a meeting that had just as much drama and even more points. UCLA trailed by 17 points after a 78-yard touchdown by USC's R. Jay Soward, with 11:06 remaining in the fourth quarter. But UCLA got a field goal, forced a punt from deep in USC territory, and drove 41 yards for a touchdown that brought the Bruins within seven points in the final three minutes. The Trojans tried to run out the clock, but UCLA forced a fumble and had the ball with 1:27 remaining and 56 yards to go. Cade McNown led the Bruins down the field and UCLA scored on a touchdown run by Skip Hicks with 39 seconds left in the game. The extra point tied the score. The two teams exchanged field goals in the first overtime, Skip Hicks ran for a 25-yard touchdown on the first play of the second overtime, and Anthony Cobbs intercepted a USC pass in the end zone to preserve the victory.

What more could you ask for than wild shootouts? Have you forgotten what city we're talking about here? This is Los Angeles. We need some stars, baby!

None of the names above could match the accolades of the key figures in the 1967 meeting.

The 1967 game featured the two best players in college football (at least according to the Heisman Trophy voters) duking it out. Gary Beban would go on to win the Heisman that year, while O. J. Simpson finished second. Simpson won it the following year.

Both of them bolstered their campaigns in that game, with Beban throwing for 301 yards and two touchdowns and Simpson rushing for 177 yards and two touchdowns.

The Bruins were ranked No. 1 in the Associated Press media and the UPI coaches polls, the Trojans were second in the UPI and fourth in the AP. The winner would go on to the Rose Bowl and a shot at the national championship.

171

And talk about the pageantry of college football. This was only the second season that ABC had televised the games in color. There couldn't be a better palette to display than the blue and gold of UCLA and the cardinal and gold of USC. (This was long before the enactment of an NCAA rule that forced the visiting team to wear white.)

UCLA led 20–14 in the fourth quarter when USC called an audible from its own 36-yard line. Quarterback Toby Page handed the ball to Simpson, who went left, cut back to the middle, and took off 64 yards for the go-ahead touchdown.

It was the signature play of Simpson's USC career and propelled the Trojans to the Rose Bowl, where they beat Indiana and were voted national champions.

Four decades later, it remains the defining game of the rivalry, a combination of big stakes, big names, and big plays that managed to top even the high standards set by this unique series.

WHO WAS USC'S GREATEST HEISMAN TROPHY WINNER?

The seven stiff-arming statues all look the same when you see them on display in Heritage Hall on the USC campus.

So how to determine which of the Heisman Trophies won by Mike Garrett, O. J. Simpson, Charles White, Marcus Allen, Carson Palmer, Matt Leinart, and Reggie Bush is the most impressive?

First of all, it can't be either of the quarterbacks, Palmer or Leinart. The University of Southern California is Tailback U, not QB Tech. So it has to be one of the five running backs.

And if you examine the numbers and the stories behind them, you'll realize it has to be Bush.

We can't go by the yardage totals. It would be unfair to Bush's predecessors because Bush played 12 regular-season games, vs. 10 for Garrett and Simpson and 11 for White and Allen. And it would be unfair to Bush, because the Trojans won seven games by 30 or more points in 2005 and he often came out of the game in the fourth quarter.

Also, Bush played in a much more pass-oriented offense.

In the 1960s, 70s, and early 80s, no USC team attempted more than 286 passes. During Bush's Heisman season the Trojans threw the ball 481 times, the second-most in school history. And when the Trojans did run the ball, they were just as likely to hand off to LenDale White as they were to Bush. Bush had 200 carries that year; White had 197.

So let's judge Bush by his yards per carry average: 8.7. The next closest Heisman winner was Charles White, at 6.2. (In fact, *LenDale* White had a better yards-per-carry average in 2005 than any of the other Heisman winners, with 6.6.)

Not only did Bush have to split running duties with LenDale White, he had to share the backfield with another Heisman Trophy winner. And after Leinart decided to come back to USC for his senior season, the coaches gave him every chance to impress the pro scouts. Leinart attempted 19 more passes than he did in his Heisman-winning 2004 season. (Bush caught 37 of them for 378 yards and two touchdowns.)

Bush managed to shine brightest amid all of the megawatts. He did it despite the fewest number of carries of USC's running back Heisman winners (about half the number of Simpson and Allen). For Bush, it was about impact more than volume. The average length of his 19 touchdown plays was 31.6 yards. White usually picked up the short-yardage scores. Bush was a threat to score from any place on the field.

One advantage Bush clearly enjoyed: the benefits of the

new millennium media. In the old days, players on the West Coast were at a distinct disadvantage when it came to the highly subjective Heisman balloting. With the bulk of the voters in the East, South, and Midwest, they rarely saw Western players, even in the early days of television. And for evening games played in the Pacific time zone, the results usually came in after newspapers on the East Coast were "put to bed," to use the journalism parlance.

That wasn't a problem for Bush. He did his thing in the era of 24-hour sports television and Internet video clips. The best example was his 513-yard, two-touchdown game against Fresno State. The game ended after 10 p.m. in Los Angeles. But it was talked about and the highlights were replayed on ESPN—even on the NFL shows—throughout the next day. That's probably what gave him the edge in the voting. Bush benefited, but so did we. We got to see every single play of the greatest USC Heisman winner of them all.

WERE THE TROJANS RIGHT TO CALL THEMSELVES BACK-TO-BACK CHAMPIONS OF THE 2003 AND 2004 SEASONS?

It was January 2006, and the Trojans found themselves in a hotly contested battle for the championship...of the 2003 season.

As USC went for its third consecutive championship (or as the locals called it in honor of the deified coach Pete Carroll—a "Three-Pete"), there was still dispute over whether their first national championship should count. We all had to revisit the tired arguments from two years before, when the voters of the Associated Press poll deemed the Trojans the top team in the country, but the computers employed by the BCS determined Louisiana State was No. 1. Never mind that the BCS system was so flawed it had to be reworked yet again, and the AP was so frustrated it disassociated itself from the BCS process and forced the would-be kingmakers to create another human poll to incorporate into their formula.

There were those, particularly in the state of Louisiana,

who insisted the Tigers had won the only championship that counted for the 2003 system.

They neglected to mention that the NCAA does not officially sanction a championship for its top-division college football. Whoever wants to crown a champion is welcome to. The BCS is just one method, not a final solution. All it could do was attempt to match the teams it determined to be No. 1 and No. 2 in a bowl game.

Any and all other techniques are just as valid. If the voters determined that USC won a championship, then it won a championship. The Associated Press had been determining champions since 1936. That's enough time to determine legitimacy.

We never got to see who would win through the normal method (i.e., a tournament) and the computers shut the Trojans out of the BCS-determined "national championship" game at the Sugar Bowl, which was played between LSU and Oklahoma. After LSU beat the Sooners and USC beat Michigan in the Rose Bowl, we were left to judge the relative merits of USC's victories over Auburn, BYU, Hawaii, Arizona State, Stanford, Notre Dame, Washington, Washington State, Arizona, and UCLA and its loss to California against LSU's victories over Louisiana-Monroe (yes, THAT Louisiana-Monroe), Arizona, Western Illinois, Georgia, Mississippi State, South Carolina, Auburn, Louisiana Tech, Alabama, Mississippi, Arkansas, and Georgia and its loss to Florida.

177

The Associated Press got it right.

And Texas made the whole three-peat argument moot by beating USC in a classic Rose Bowl game on January 4, 2006.

The Longhorns were clearly the champions of the 2005 season, for once providing a clear-cut answer in college football. But that wasn't enough for some fans. Pushed over the edge by ESPN's relentless hype of USC in the leadup to the Rose Bowl, they set up a website called onepeat.com and raised funds to pay for a billboard that read "Shouldn't Dynasties Win More Than One?" Across the bottom of the billboard it read: "LSU '03 USC '04 Texas '05"

They spent $5,000 on this. That's $5,000 wasted on a flawed premise: that a legitimate champion isn't a champion.

USC doesn't have to apologize for its 2003 championship. But only in college football would they have to spend more than one season defending it.

SHOULD PETE CARROLL HAVE GONE FOR IT IN THE 2006 ROSE BOWL?

One decision . . . two yards . . . a third consecutive national championship on the line . . . fourth down.

For Pete Carroll, it would become the single most-scrutinized decision in his tenure as USC's coach. He stayed true to what had gotten him to this point. He made the right call. He went for it.

The 2006 Rose Bowl turned out to be worth all of the endless hype that preceded the matchup between the top-ranked Trojans and the No. 2 Texas Longhorns.

An offensive explosion saw the Trojans turn a 16–10 half-time deficit into a 38–26 lead in the fourth quarter. But Texas quarterback Vince Young led a 69-yard drive for a touchdown and extra point that brought the Longhorns to within five.

With 2:13 left in the game, USC faced fourth-and-two on the Texas 45-yard line. One thing had been established at this point: USC could not stop Young. He was picking the Trojans apart with short passes, or making them look foolish whenever he ran. The choices were trying to make it a little more difficult for him by adding another 25 to 40 yards to his drive, or trying to take him out of the picture completely by picking up a first down and milking the clock. The risk there was giving him the ball near midfield with more than 2 minutes to work with. That would be like a scrimmage for Young.

Carroll decided to put the game in the hands of his offense. It might have been tough for a man who rose to NFL coaching prominence on the defensive side of the ball. But, for maybe the first time in his time at USC, Carroll didn't have an answer for an opponent. Nothing they had prepared for Young worked, and they couldn't make any in-game adjustments.

It wasn't as if Texas had an answer for USC's high-powered offense. The Trojans had rolled up over 500 yards at that point.

And Carroll was doing what he'd done all season, what he'd done since he got too conservative in USC's last loss 35 games ago. He was playing aggressively. The Trojans had won back-to-back national championships with that mindset and stood on the verge of a third.

He had done it earlier in this game, with mixed results. On fourth-and-one from the Texas 18 in the first quarter, the Trojans tried a quarterback sneak with Matt Leinart that was stopped short. In the third quarter, the Trojans had fourth-and-one at the Texas 12 and handed off to LenDale White, who stormed all the way to the end zone.

Carroll was doing what he always did. The worst thing a coach can do is change his approach in the biggest tests.

You wouldn't see an R&B singer choose a country tune in the final round of *American Idol*, would you?

It was the right move. But once Carroll made the decision, he might have erred in letting his rookie offensive coordinator, Lane Kiffin, call the play. Carroll had taken a more active role on the offensive side of the ball even with the respected Norm Chow around the year before, but this moment was all Kiffin. Kiffin went with 27 Power Quad, a play that didn't even have Heisman Trophy winner Reggie Bush on the field.

Even if the bigger White made for a better short-yardage runner, the Trojans might have at least lined Bush up as a receiver. Not only was Bush the nation's best player with the ball in his hands, he also served as the most effective decoy. Kiffin would say later that Texas wouldn't have covered him, that all of the defenders were lined up to play the run.

That's exactly what the Longhorns got, with White trying to move to the left. They stopped him a yard short, and had the ball on their own 44 with 2:09 remaining. That was more than enough time for Young to take a samurai sword to the USC defense and score the winning touchdown.

Carroll's consolation? Young probably would have done it anyway, no matter where the drive began. The only way to be assured of stopping him was to never let him start. The only way to do that was to go for it on fourth down.

WHAT WAS THE BEST USC–NOTRE DAME GAME?

Believe it or not, for a rivalry that was formed on a train ride in 1925 and has been contested more than 80 times, you don't have to delve that deep into history to find the best game.

USC vs. Notre Dame—dubbed college football's greatest intersectional rivalry— started because the USC athletic director's wife chatted up legendary Notre Dame coach Knute Rockne's wife during a trip to South Bend, Indiana. It was the women who successfully sold Rockne on the idea of making the game an annual affair.

Through the years, the rivalry has featured USC's 55 straight points in 1974, a last-second field goal by Notre Dame's John Carney in 1986, an overtime touchdown pass from Brad Otten to Rodney Sermons in 1996, Rod Sherman's 15-yard touchdown reception to knock off an unbeaten Irish team in 1964, and Notre Dame's 22 unanswered points to win in 1999.

But the best of the bunch was USC's victorious touchdown on the final play of the game in 2005. It was a game that drained players from their helmets to their cleats. It featured big plays and even a little controversy. It must have been special because the Irish broke out their green jerseys. Gotta love the green jerseys.

This was the game that brought the rivalry back to the rivalry. With Coach Pete Carroll getting the program back on track, USC had won the previous three meetings by scores of 44–13, 45–14, and 41–10. It didn't take a math major to see the trend developing there.

But in 2006, Charlie Weis' first year as head coach, Notre Dame had a renewed offense, and the Irish were ranked ninth by the Associated Press. Quarterback Brady Quinn was on his way to becoming a first-round draft pick. The coaching matchup was one of the game's biggest subplots, as the former offensive coordinator for the Super Bowl champion New England Patriots squared off against Carroll, the former New York Jets defensive coordinator and head coach of the Jets and Patriots.

As it turned out, Notre Dame scored more points than any USC opponent during the 27-game winning streak and dominated the time of possession almost 2 to 1. The high-powered Trojan offense, meanwhile, scored only 14 points through the first 2 ½ quarters.

But Reggie Bush broke loose for a 45-yard touchdown run in the third quarter to tie the score at 21–21. Another Bush touchdown in the fourth quarter put the Trojans ahead, 27–24. But Quinn brought the Irish back and scored on a 5-yard run with 2:04 left in the game.

That set the stage for two of the most memorable plays in USC history.

The first came when USC faced fourth-and-nine at its own

26. All of a sudden the winning streak, the No. 1 ranking, and the chance for a third consecutive national championship were down to one play. And quarterback Matt Leinart called an audible. Instead of a slant or an out pattern, Leinart sent wide receiver Dwayne Jarrett deep down the sidelines, and Leinart dropped the ball right in his lap for a 61-yard gain. It was an audacious clutch play, the type that lived up to the swagger the Trojans had developed under Carroll.

The Trojans got the ball to the Notre Dame 2-yard line in the next four plays, then Leinart tried to make a dash for the end zone. He was stopped short and the ball flew out of bounds. Believe it or not, the Trojans caught a break at Notre Dame Stadium. The officials ruled that the ball went out of bounds at the 1-yard line with one second remaining on the clock, and the Trojans had one more play.

They called a quarterback sneak for Leinart. His initial push was stopped, but Bush ran up to give Leinart a friendly shove, and the two tumbled into the end zone.

Was the push illegal? Yes. But it wasn't called. And perhaps it was deemed a karmic trade-off for the way Notre Dame let the field grow longer than the rough at the U.S. Open in an attempt to slow down the Trojans' speed.

The Trojans and their fans who made the trek to South Bend were deliriously happy. This was the type of game that makes college football so wonderful, and reminds us that USC–Notre Dame is as good as anything the sport has to offer.

WHY ISN'T UCLA FOOTBALL LIKE USC FOOTBALL?

UCLA, like USC, is in a warm-weather climate, which should make it attractive to recruits.

UCLA is in the same city as USC. In fact, it's in a nicer part of town…and closer to the ocean, so the afternoon breezes can keep it cooler than USC's campus during those summer afternoon training camp sessions.

UCLA, like USC, is in the middle of one of the most fertile prep school football breeding grounds in the country.

Yet UCLA hasn't won a football national championship since 1954, while USC has racked up seven in that span, while hauling in gluttonous recruiting classes that pack in prospects at the rate Starbucks adds new stores.

Why such a disparity for two schools only 13 miles apart?

College sports are all about recruiting, and recruiting is a funny business based on perception. Remember, we're talking about the preferences of 17- and 18-year-olds here.

But there are structural disadvantages working against UCLA in the recruiting game. First off is the home stadium. Kids want to play in the Rose Bowl on New Year's Day, not on the first Saturday in September with half-empty stands because students haven't returned for the fall semester yet.

Almost all of the top football programs play in a campus stadium (Miami is a notable exception). Technically, the Coliseum isn't on USC's campus, but it's right across the street. And since the Rams, Raiders, and UCLA have vacated it, it is identified only with USC. Every memorable home game the Trojans have played was in that big oval. All of the biggest names in the program's history have walked through that tunnel behind the end zone. The place oozes with tradition.

The Rose Bowl doesn't scream "UCLA!" And by being so far from campus, it's hard to replicate the college atmosphere. It's kind of like trying to throw a frat party in a bank.

And when they are on campus, UCLA football players will always feel secondary to the basketball players. Athletes want to feel like they're "The Man." UCLA's favorite sons play in Pauley Pavilion, where all the championship banners hang. On campus, of course.

The alumni care more about the basketball team as well. If they go too long between Final Four appearances they get grumpy. Meanwhile, making a run at a national championship once every decade or so is enough to keep the football fans satisfied. Steve Lavin won 65 percent of the basketball games he coached at UCLA and was fired after seven years. Terry Donahue won 67 percent of his football games and lasted 20 years. The basketball job turned over five times during his tenure.

Bruin fans are growing increasingly restless, however, as they watch USC return to its football glory, often at UCLA's expense. They grew impatient with Karl Dorrell quickly, circulated petitions to get him fired, and were only temporarily pacified when UCLA upset USC in the final regular season game of 2006.

But sometimes paying too much attention to the football program can backfire. UCLA doesn't do a good enough job of damage control on its incidents. Any program is subject to having players get into fights, or get arrested. USC seems to sweep the stories into the corner when no one's looking, while UCLA's incidents stay in the news. A great example was the handicapped parking scandal in 1999.

Even the facts were misconstrued. It wasn't that able-bodied football players were using illegally obtained handicapped-parking placards to park in the coveted blue spots. They took advantage of their football injuries to obtain the placards for their temporary "disabled" condition. Mostly the placards allowed them to park in metered spots for as long as they wanted without having to drop coins in the meter. Instead, everyone pictured linebackers parking right next to a building while a woman in a wheelchair had to park down the street.

USC has had players deck other students, players accept forbidden contributions from agents, and players flirt with (and sometimes succumb to) academic ineligibility. None of it seems to dull the glow that emanates from head coach Pete Carroll.

The USC fan base grants Carroll immunity from any challenge because he restored what Trojans fans view as the natural order in town.

UCLA had the advantage in the 1990s, winning the cross-town rivalry game eight straight times and coming within a game of playing for the national championship in 1998. But since Carroll's arrival, it's advantage USC. When things go right at USC, the well practically refills itself. And at the moment there are too many physical and philosophical roadblocks for UCLA to compete.

WHAT WAS THE GREATEST UCLA BASKETBALL TEAM?

 77

If we had to select just one of the 11 men's basketball championship banners hanging in Pauley Pavilion, which would it be?

No easy answers here. More research just brings more options. You figure you'd start with the Lew Alcindor-era and the Bill Walton-era teams and pick between them. But even choosing among Alcindor's three championship teams and Walton's two title squads is difficult.

Walton was at his personal best in the 1973 championship game, setting a scoring record with 44 points that still stands today. But the 1972 team had the highest scoring average of any of the championship teams.

Then again, Alcindor's 1968 team set a school record with 1,161 field goals. But Alcindor's best scoring season (and the best in UCLA history) was 1967, when he averaged 29 points per game.

And which team scored the most points in a Final Four game? Well, it's none of the above: the 1965 team scored 108 points against Wichita State.

Still, would you want to take a team whose tallest player

was 6-foot-5 against a team with either Walton or Alcindor? Didn't think so.

That's why we have to come back to one of their teams. Walton might be the most fundamentally sound big man in college basketball history. And even though he played before freshmen were eligible for the varsity team, Walton's school record of 1,370 career rebounds still stands.

But Alcindor (now known as Kareem Abdul-Jabbar) was one of the most dominant forces in the game's history. Opponents feared driving against him; not only could he block your shot, there was a chance he might just catch it in mid-air. And it's amazing he scored as many points as he did (2,325) despite playing against zone defenses and stall offenses both designed to keep the ball out of his hands.

The greatest player doesn't always make for the greatest team, but in Alcindor's case he had a strong supporting cast. In fact, in 1968 Lucius Allen and Mike Warren joined Alcindor on the All-American first team, the only time in school history that three members were simultaneously honored.

And that's what makes the 1968 team the best of the Bruins. They had everything you could want from a team. It returned four of the five starters from the undefeated 1967 team. A year's worth of experience meant the 1968 team was savvier. It had to be, since the NCAA outlawed the dunk, depriving Alcindor and the Bruins of the easiest two points in college basketball.

When you're filling out your NCAA tournament brackets, it's wise to look for good guard play, and that's what the 1968 team had with Allen and Warren in the backcourt. They had Lynn Shackelford knocking down outside shots. And Mike Lynn gave them a fifth starter who averaged double-digit scoring.

The 1968 team wasn't perfect, but it had an excuse: Alcindor had an injured eye when the Bruins lost to Houston in a history-making game in the Astrodome, a nationally televised contest that was played in front of a crowd of almost 53,000 people, showing college basketball could be almost as popular as football. With Alcindor back at full strength, UCLA destroyed Houston in a Final Four rematch, 101–69.

So the team wasn't unblemished, but it was at its best when it mattered most. That's the essence of a John Wooden-coached team, and this one epitomized it.

WHAT WERE JOHN WOODEN'S FAVORITE UCLA TEAMS?

You could never get John Wooden to say which of the 10 national championship teams he coached was the best.

He has, on occasion, given his *favorite* teams: the first one in 1964, with no player over 6-foot-5, which wound up with a 30–0 record, was one. "The smallest team that ever won, the shortest team that ever will win, in my opinion," Wooden said.

Next was the 1970 team that won a championship in the first "Year Without"—as in, without Lew Alcindor.

"After his senior year, there were coaches and media that one way or another implied, 'They're going to get their come-uppance now that the big guy is gone,'" Wooden said. "We won the next four in a row and five of the next six after he left. That's a pretty good come-uppance."

And finally there was his final team, the one that sent him out a winner in 1975.

"I announced my retirement a couple of days before, and it's nice to go out with a championship," Wooden said.

DID THE ROSE BOWL DO THE RIGHT THING BY JOINING THE BCS?

 Something changed when Miami and Nebraska took the field for the 88th Rose Bowl in 2002.

For the first time since 1947, it wasn't a team from the Big Ten playing a team from the Pacific-10 (or its forerunner, the Pacific Coast Conference).

Instead, it was the Hurricanes and the Cornhuskers, a matchup determined by a computer and dumped on the Rose Bowl's doorstep. The game lacked competitiveness in addition to lacking tradition. It was the reward the Rose Bowl received for joining the BCS and getting the right to host the so-called national championship game once every four years.

But as it turned out, it was the right move to make.

The Rose Bowl tried to have it both ways, to get its shot at the national championship and retain the traditional Pac-10 vs. Big Ten matchup in the other three years while it awaited its next turn at the big game, but found it was just as easy to fall victim to the BCS selection process. In 2003, while the Orange Bowl hosted what appeared to be a Rose

Bowl-suited USC vs. Iowa game, Oklahoma and Washington State came to Pasadena. The teams were greeted by a sight almost as rare as rain in Southern California on New Year's Day: rows of empty seats in the stadium.

There have been other slaps to the face of the Granddaddy of them all, including the notion of Pacific-10 champions having to "settle" for playing in the Rose Bowl. That was the scenario that unfolded when UCLA upset USC in the final game of the 2006 season. The Trojans took the No. 2 ranking into the game and were in line for an invitation to the "national championship" game at the Fiesta Bowl if they won. When they lost, their consolation was that they'd still get a trip to the Rose Bowl as the Pac-10 representative. Their opponents: a Michigan team that was limping to Pasadena after losing the annual rivalry matchup to Ohio State—which had the added bonus of a BCS championship invitation on the line for the winner. The Rose Bowl had been reduced to a parting gift.

There are those who believed the Rose Bowl sold its soul when it joined the BCS, that it would be better off standing on the outside and retaining its tradition and dignity. But they aren't acknowledging the changing face of college football, and haven't come to the realization that it's better to be diminished than completely irrelevant.

The irony of the BCS is that while it ostensibly preserves the bowl concept and can create more than 30 "winners" at the end of the season, it has actually reduced college football's postseason to No. 1 vs. No. 2 and everything else. Ratings for the non-championship games are dropping, as only fans of the teams involved see them as anything but glorified exhibition games.

By steadfastly putting the old ways ahead of everything else, the Rose Bowl would soon find itself on the same road to irrelevance as the Cotton Bowl, which was once one of the biggest New Year's Day games, but found itself on the outside of the BCS.

By joining the BCS, the Rose Bowl can at least be the focal point every four years, when its turn in the rotation comes up. And now, with the concept of double hosting, the Rose Bowl has a chance of preserving its traditional matchup even in the years it hosts the championship game. In 2006, the first year of such an idea, the Fiesta Bowl had the ultra-exciting Boise State–Oklahoma game on January 1, in addition to the big showdown between Ohio State and Florida a week later.

And after an awkward introduction to the BCS world, the Rose Bowl bounced back nicely, with a 2004 USC-Michigan game that helped the Trojans win the Associated Press national championship, a 2005 breakout performance by Texas quarterback Vince Young in a shootout with Michigan, followed by an even better show in 2006 by Young against USC in one of the greatest college football games ever played.

As grand as the Rose Bowl tradition is, it would have to go if the college presidents ever came to their senses and approved a Division I-A playoff. And if the presidents did catch a case of the smarts, they would have to utilize the Rose Bowl stadium as part of any postseason plan.

One thing that isn't up for argument even in the debate-filled world of college football: There's no better venue for a game than the Rose Bowl on a sunny day with its mountain backdrop...no matter which teams are on the field.

HOCKEY

WHAT WAS THE LONG-TERM IMPACT OF THE WAYNE GRETZKY TRADE?

Wayne Gretzky brought the Stanley Cup to Los Angeles. He didn't win it during the eight years he played for the Kings, but if you looked closely, you could find Gretzky's fingerprints on the well-polished Cup when the Anaheim Ducks raised it over their heads in June of 2007.

August 9, 1988, goes down as one of the most significant dates in sports history. That's the day the Edmonton Oilers traded Wayne Gretzky to the Kings. (The other, mostly forgotten, parts of the trade: Marty McSorley and Mike Krushelnyski came with Gretzky to the Kings and Jimmy Carson, Martin Gelinas, three first-round draft picks, and $15 million went to Edmonton.)

Before Gretzky, Los Angeles was a hockey outpost. The Forum was half-empty on most nights for the first five years after the Kings began play in 1967. Jack Kent Cooke, the Kings' original owner, once said, "I think the 600,000 Canadians who relocated to Southern California came here to get away from hockey."

Thanks to Gretzky, we learned that hockey can sell in sunny cities. Attendance jumped by more than 3,000 per game in Gretzky's first year in L.A. In 1991–92 the Kings sold out the entire season, packing the Forum with 16,005 fans every night. (It didn't hurt that Gretzky's arrival coincided with the Kings' switch to a black-and-white color scheme AND the rise of West Coast gangsta rappers who liked to wear Kings gear in their videos.)

And so the great expansion and migration to the so-called Sun Belt was on: the Sharks (with their hockey stick-chewing logo) in San Jose, the Panthers in Miami, the Lightning in Tampa Bay, and the Hurricanes in North Carolina. The Winnipeg Jets moved to Phoenix and became the Coyotes. The Minnesota North Stars moved to Dallas—and dropped the "North."

But the strongest statement of all, that the Southland market could support two NHL teams, came when the Ducks came into existence in 1993.

A combination of needs was in play. The new arena going up in Anaheim needed a primary tenant. Disney wanted another marketing measure. And Kings owner Bruce McNall wanted the cash infusion the territorial rights fee from an expansion team would bring.

So in came the Mighty Ducks of Anaheim. (At first, people thought Disney CEO Michael Eisner was kidding when he said they would name the team after Disney's "Mighty Ducks" movie.)

But none of it would have happened if Wayne Gretzky had not sold tickets.

199

"He's the reason we have a hockey team in Anaheim," Ducks forward Teemu Selanne said in a *USA Today* article. McNall added: "There's no way that I could have gotten Disney to even look at having a team if not for all the excitement that Wayne created."

Now, a generation after Gretzky arrived, we're seeing the effect he had on a grassroots level. Southern California-bred hockey players are popping up with increasing frequency in the NHL draft, and in March of 2007, Noah Clarke, of La Verne, became the first Southern California native to score a goal for the Kings.

If Gretzky represented a giant leap forward, the NHL lockouts of 1994 and 2004 represented two inept stumbles backward. The first full season after the 1994 lockout—and the first season after Gretsky's trade to St. Louis—Kings attendance dropped by 2,000 per game. When the entire 2004–05 season was shut down, it seemed to wipe hockey off the sports landscape. Well, you could still see it, but you had to look deep in the bins, behind Ultimate Fighting and the X Games.

We also learned the Orange County market isn't dedicated to hockey no matter what. Once the novelty of the Mighty Ducks wore off—and their playoff appearance in Year 4 became a memory—the Ducks dropped to last in the NHL in attendance in 2001–02, when they averaged 12,002 per game. Disney wanted out, and eventually sold to Orange County billionaire Henry Samueli in 2005.

He took out the Mighty, changed the colors, and watched the Ducks take the Cup. But the origins all go back to Gretzky.

He was the perfect salesman for Los Angeles, a superstar in a city that worships celebrity. But the other thing this area responds to is a winner. Now we'll see if a Stanley Cup has the same impact as one Wayne Gretzky.

WHO IS THE KING OF THE KINGS?

 What do you get when you combine the long-time Kings production of Marcel Dionne with the ambassador skills of Wayne Gretzky? The answer is Luc Robitaille.

Gretzky is the greatest player who ever played for the Kings, but he isn't the greatest King. Gretzky's best years—and the bulk of his 894 career goals—came with the Edmonton Oilers.

For years, Dionne stood as the goal-scoring standard for the Kings (and his 731 career goals rank fourth in NHL history). But on January 19, 2006, Robitaille passed Dionne's franchise record when he scored his 551st goal as a King.

Even though Dionne is one of the all-time greats in his sport, he could walk down Hollywood Boulevard without getting noticed. He was an almost invisible superstar.

While Robitaille never had the coast-to-coast fame of Gretzky, he did his best to carry out the Great One's goal of bringing the sport to the masses when Robitaille returned to a Gretzky-less Kings squad in 1997.

Whether it was appearances on behalf of the team, interviews with every media outlet, or sticking around to sign that extra autograph, Robitaille became the face of the franchise around the turn of the 21st century.

"I don't take [the fans] for granted," Robitaille told Kingshockey.com. "I know that I've always gone out of my way. I've never said no, although there were some times where I was in a hurry and had to walk away, for autographs. I've always spent time trying to develop hockey in this community and teach young kids that it is possible to do your dream, whatever it is. I've always taken pride in trying not to say no."

Robitaille understood hockey's precarious place in the United States sports pecking order. Unfortunately, he had a better grasp of the concept than hockey's so-called leadership. When the lockout wiped out the 2004–05 season, Robitaille held a news conference at his house.

"I think we're killing the game," he said.

One thing that never died was the fans' love for Robitaille. It all came pouring out in his final game at the end of the 2005–06 season. The Staples Center fans showered him with chants of "Luuuuuuuuuc!" They gave him repeated standing ovations.

Even when Robitaille was away from the Kings, Los Angeles was never far from his heart. When he won the championship with the Detroit Red Wings in 2002, he brought the Stanley Cup back to Los Angeles for a tour of the city, bringing it to Dodger Stadium and up to the hills for a photo op with the Hollywood sign. And when he was a free agent at the end of his career, he came back to the same city where it began 19 years earlier.

He came into the NHL as a ninth-round pick, considered by many observers to be too slow to make it in the league. What he lacked in speed he more than made up for with stick skills, using his sniper-accurate shot to score 668 goals and become the highest-scoring left wing in NHL history.

After he retired, he joined the Kings' front office and a year later was named the club's president of business operations. His next phase is reminiscent of Dave Taylor, who spent 17 years on the ice with the Kings and 10 years as the team's general manager.

When it's over, you'll be able to say no one served the Kings any better than Luc Robitaille.

WHICH DUCK FLIES THE HIGHEST?

Sure, Ducks fans could appreciate the significance of the moment when Scott Niedermayer passed the Stanley Cup to his brother Rob. Great story, the siblings sharing this triumph, finally celebrating together four years after Scott's New Jersey Devils beat Rob's Ducks in the Stanley Cup finals.

But the loudest cheers came when Teemu Selanne raised the Cup over his head. Selanne has become the Definitive Duck, the man most identifiable with the franchise.

When the Ducks acquired him in a trade with the Winnipeg Jets on February 7, 1996, Selanne helped bring credibility to a team that was named after a movie, had a duck-billed goalie mask for a logo, and wore the colors of jade and eggplant. Selanne was just three seasons removed from the most prolific goal-scoring rookie year in NHL history. He scored 76 goals in 1992–93. The top three Ducks scorers in the team's inaugural season the next year combined for 62 goals.

Paul Kariya arrived in Anaheim before Selanne, and at times Kariya's dazzling skills shined brighter. But Selanne's easy-going nature made sure there wouldn't be a repeat of the attention battles that strained the Lakers franchise.

Instead, Selanne was attached to Kariya. When Kariya ended a bitter contract holdout in 1996, Selanne looked like a kid who had just been excused from school to head to the ice cream parlor. Seven years later, after a three-year stint in San Jose, Selanne would join Kariya for a year in Colorado, the two signing free-agent contracts below market value in an effort to win a Stanley Cup together.

Not only did they fall short, but Selanne had his worst season. An injured left knee deprived him of his famous speed, and he scored only 16 goals. Then came the NHL lockout...which wound up being the best thing that could have happened to him at that time. He had reconstructive surgery on his knee and had a full season to rehab. When the NHL reopened for business, Selanne returned to the Ducks—and to form. He put together the two greatest back-to-back goal-scoring seasons ever by a player in his mid-30s.

He also took over the Ducks record books, becoming the first player in franchise history to pass the 300-goal mark. A decade after he set the team record for single-season goals (52) and points (109), Selanne finished third in the NHL with 48 goals.

Still, you could argue that by 2007 Jean-Sebastien Giguere had become a more valuable member of the Ducks. Every Stanley Cup contender needs a goaltender who is capable of carrying a team for two months. Giguere showed he could do it in his rookie season, when he played so well he won the Conn Smythe Trophy as the playoff MVP even though the Ducks lost in the Stanley Cup finals. Giguere was solid again in the 2007 run, with a 1.97 goals-against average.

But the emotional center of the team was Selanne. Ask a Duck who he wanted to see win the Cup the most and he was likely to say Selanne even more than himself.

And the player known for his speed and skill even came to epitomize the tough-guy attitude of the Ducks and their new dark uniforms. During the playoffs, his face was filled with bruises and cuts that required a total of 20 stitches to close (OK, so perhaps the origins—including a puck in the face during warm-ups and a run-in with teammate Chris Pronger's stick—didn't always sound like worthy battle tales).

He was there when the Ducks were Mighty. More than that, he was there when the Ducks were excellent. No other player is such an integral part of the franchise's history.

WILL HOCKEY MATTER IN LOS ANGELES AGAIN?

83 On June 9, 2007, the Anaheim Ducks gathered to celebrate the Stanley Cup championship with their fans, in the parking lot outside the Honda Center that rocked throughout the playoffs.

The Cup itself was flown in a helicopter, to the musical accompaniment of "Ride of the Valkyries" (think "Apocalypse Now"). There were free hot dogs. Fans didn't have to pay for parking.

And only 15,000 people showed up, a smaller crowd than the customers who had to pay to get inside the arena for the games. This was on a Saturday evening.

By comparison, when the Angels won the World Series in 2002, city officials estimated that a combined 100,000 watched the team's parade down Disneyland's Main Street and subsequent rally outside the stadium . . . on a Tuesday afternoon.

The day after the Ducks won the Cup, the L.A. sports radio shows devoted a segment to them. Then the hosts went back to talking about Kobe Bryant and Paris Hilton.

So if the first possession of the cherished Stanley Cup by a California team can't drive the locals into a hockey frenzy, what will?

This was another sign that Los Angeles might be immune to several national trends—a steep drop in housing prices, for one—but one malaise that caught on was America's growing disinterest in hockey.

In the 2006–07 season, the *Los Angeles Times* stopped sending its hockey beat writers on the road with the team for most away games. You can argue in circles about whether lack of coverage is a cause of lack of interest in hockey or a result of it, but we do know this: Less is not better.

Much of the blame originates in Commissioner Gary Bettman's office at NHL headquarters in New York. Twice he failed to avert league-wide lockouts, and as a result, the league suffered two deep wounds. In 1994, when the first half of the season was wiped out, he lost the momentum from the New York Rangers' ending their 44-year Stanley Cup drought thanks to their charismatic leader, Mark Messier. Big news in New York tends to become big news nationally. But three months later there was no hockey news at all except dull talk about collective bargaining negotiations.

And don't forget it was only a year and a half from the Kings' run to the Stanley Cup finals, the high-water mark for hockey interest in Los Angeles. Luc Robitaille was traded in the summer of 1994, Wayne Gretzky was traded to St. Louis in February of 1996, and the Kings didn't make it back to the playoffs until 1998.

The Kings' slide back to mediocrity is another reason for the lack of interest in Southern California. They have the oldest and largest hockey fan base in California, but have had so little to cheer. If the die-hards can't get enthusiastic, how is the casual fan supposed to hop on the bandwagon?

It doesn't look like the Kings will be leading hockey out of the darkness, either. The ownership group seems preoccupied with its various sports and multi-use facilities around the world, and has never made a big-splash move in hockey on par with the signing of David Beckham for the soccer Galaxy.

That leaves the Ducks. The good news is they won the Stanley Cup, and then re-signed goaltender Jean-Sebastien Giguere. They sold out their final 22 games of the 2006–07 regular season and every playoff game. The Stanley Cup-clinching game did decent TV numbers in Los Angeles, with a 6.0 local rating and a 12 share. The excitement brought season-ticket sales and renewals for the next year to 14,000.

The bad news? That's about as many people as showed up for the Cup rally. In Los Angeles, that doesn't qualify as a phenomenon. And it's nowhere near the number of spectators who would come to the parking lot if Paris Hilton and Lindsay Lohan were having a drag race.

The Cup found a home in Southern California. But we learned that home is in a two-bedroom apartment, with no chance of expansion.

OTHER SPORTS

IF L.A. IS SO CAR-CRAZED, WHY ISN'T NASCAR MORE POPULAR HERE?

In Los Angeles, cars aren't just transportation; they're status symbols, lifestyle choices, and means of empowerment. L.A. residents wash their cars obsessively and replace them before the tires are worn. They love cars. They just don't seem overly preoccupied with hopping in their cars to go watch other cars make left turns around an oval.

NASCAR's failure to captivate the Los Angeles market has been the equivalent of a yellow flag in stock car racing's road to world domination.

The California Speedway has been a part of the NASCAR cup circuit since 1997. In 2004 it received a second race, taking it away from Darlington Raceway in South Carolina. (To racing fans, that was the equivalent of moving a college basketball game from Cameron Indoor Stadium and playing it in the Alamodome.) Ever since the California Speedway got the double-dip, it hasn't sold out either of them.

At first, it's hard to believe NASCAR hasn't clicked here. There's interest from the top in Hollywood, with stars such as Tom Cruise (*Days of Thunder*) and Will Ferrell (*Talladega Nights: The Ballad of Ricky Bobby*) making NASCAR-themed movies. And if you look closely enough, you'll see a Dale Earnhardt No. 3 sticker on cars (granted, not on any of the countless Mercedes driving around town).

And it's not the lack of talent. NASCAR isn't like the golf or tennis tours, where event organizers are at the mercy of the stars' schedules and preferences. If Tiger Woods or the Williams sisters don't show up at your event, you might as well give tickets away at the grocery store. But with NASCAR you get every driver every week. Dale Earnhardt Jr., Jeff Gordon, Tony Stewart—they'll all be in action, as close to a guarantee as you'll get in sports.

Even with the star power, the NASCAR races don't have the feel of a must-see event. Additional food and entertainment options at the Speedway have not provided an attendance boost, either.

The first problem is, the races aren't in Los Angeles. They're in Fontana. Not many folks who live in the 310 or 323 area codes feel like driving an hour east of downtown to do anything. These days they don't even drive past Fontana to go to Palm Springs, that former Hollywood retreat. Any eastward travel is likely to be made by jet to Las Vegas. The irony is the diminished enthusiasm for the race has actually made it easier to drive there, because the traffic heading to the track isn't as bad.

Even those who don't mind the driving can't feel good about the weather. It can be overcast or even rainy during the first race in February, and unbearably hot during the second race over the Labor Day weekend.

For race aficionados, the layout of the Speedway doesn't lend itself to frequent passing or good old paint-swappin'.

People in the area have an appreciation for car events. The Long Beach Grand Prix, for all of its transformations and permutations over the years, had one of its most successful weekends in recent years in 2007. They have managed to sell it as more than a race; it's a weekend event in a seaside city.

The Speedway is still capable of drawing 80,000 to 90,000 to a NASCAR race. It's just a matter of finding those fringe fans that would fill every last seat.

Or maybe there's another lesson here: If you're having trouble bringing Los Angeles people to the race, you might be better off bringing the race to Los Angeles.

How about converting the land being used for a track that's doing even worse—Hollywood Park—into a track for cars in the middle of a city that loves automobiles?

SAMPRAS OR TIGER?

85

Sampras and Tiger: two entries under the "local boy does good" category.

Pete Sampras was born in Washington, D.C., but his family moved to Palos Verdes when he was 7, and that's where his tennis game began to blossom. He went on to win a record 14 Grand Slam events in his professional career.

Tiger Woods was born and raised in Cypress, where he spent hours practicing at the Navy Golf Club. He is on pace to surpass Jack Nicklaus' record of 18 majors.

So which is the greater accomplishment? Let's break it down by category:

FORMAT

Tennis tournaments are seeded, providing an easier path to the final for those with the best prior accomplishments. In golf, no one starts out with a schedule advantage. The desirable later starting times for the final two rounds are earned by early round performance within that tournament.

Advantage: Woods.

MARGIN FOR ERROR

Golfers can recover from an off day in the early rounds if they come back and shoot lower scores in the following days. Woods has shot an opening round in the 70s five times in the majors (including a 74 at the 2005 Masters) and rallied to win the tournament. A slipup at the start of a tennis tournament means elimination.

Advantage: Sampras

THE FIELD

Sampras rose to prominence as the John McEnroe–Ivan Lendl era was finishing, and his heyday ended before Roger Federer arrived on the scene. The only great opponent in his prime that Sampras faced was Andre Agassi, but Agassi had his personal struggles with inconsistency that took him in and out of tennis' top 10. Woods has fended off the likes of Phil Mickelson, Ernie Els, and Vijay Singh.

Advantage: Woods

DIFFERENT DOMAINS

Sampras won Grand Slams, as the big tennis tournaments are called, but he never won The Grand Slam: taking the Australian Open, the French Open, Wimbledon, and the U.S. Open in the same year. And he never won the clay-court French, denying him the career Grand Slam that rival Agassi captured. If you twist the semantics, Woods did get a Grand Slam, holding the Masters, U.S. Open, British Open, and PGA Championship trophies simultaneously, although he didn't win them all in the same calendar year. But he has won every major at least twice in his career, showing he can handle everything from the lengthy rough of the U.S. Open to the wind and bunkers of the British.

Advantage: Woods.

CAREER LIFE SPAN

Sampras didn't have much time to get his work done. Age 30 is often the beginning of the end for tennis players; Sampras retired at 32. At that age, many golfers are just getting started. They benefit from experience, especially when they make repeated trips to the same course. Woods will probably play 80 competitive rounds at Augusta National by the time he's done. He'll know the putting lines better than the oldest caddies. Neither sport is played with a clock, but Sampras was the one who had to beat the buzzer.

Advantage: Sampras.

And so, a little surprisingly, the overall edge goes to Sampras. That's probably the way it should be right now. Sampras is the record-holder, while Woods still has some work to do.

WHAT WAS THE GREATEST SPORTS FEAT AT STAPLES CENTER?

For a building that's only been open since 1999, Staples Center has seen an abundance of big games and special moments.

The Lakers and Sparks have hoisted a combined five championship banners there. Kobe Bryant went for 81 points on the court. Shane Mosley outboxed Oscar De La Hoya in the building's first fight. The Kings had their Flurry on Figueroa. Staples Center even played host to that rarest of sights, a Clippers second-round playoff game.

None of those amazing moments ushered in a new era in their sport, or expanded the envelope of competition. That's what Travis Pastrana accomplished when he pulled off a double back flip on his motorcycle in the X Games on August 4, 2006: a stunning sight of man and machine in unison, hurtling through the air.

It wasn't the first time Pastrana had done the stunt in competition. He landed it in the Moto X games in Spokane, Washington, earlier that year.

But these were the X Games, the World Series of extreme

sports. In fact, they used to be called the Extreme Games, when they started off in Providence, Rhode Island, in 1995. Creating this sports festival of BMX bikes, skateboards, and motorcycles was one of the smarter things ESPN ever did. Remember, televised sports is all about advertising, and if the NFL is the perfect vehicle for brewing companies to market beer, the X Games could provide the target audience to sell Mountain Dew.

It was such a hit, with 198,000 showing up in Providence, that it immediately became an annual event instead of biannual as originally planned. In 2003 the X Games (renamed to sound snappier) came to Staples Center for the first time. Los Angeles, whose oceanside cities created the skateboarding craze, made a natural setting for the event.

Skater icon Tony Hawk created the signature moment of those 2003 Games when he pulled off a 900—a two-and-a-half rotation spin.

But it was more breathtaking to watch Pastrana somersaulting through the air with his motorcycle four years later. And we can all recognize that anytime you double the previous standard, you've done more than just set a record. It had been six years since Carey Hart first did a motorcycle back flip in competition. For Pastrana to add a second flip was like an NBA player topping Wilt Chamberlain's single-game record by scoring 200 points.

Pastrana had claimed that he wouldn't try the double back flip again after Spokane, but in the practice sessions leading up to X Games 12, he was working on it. He also wanted the "kicker" that would launch him in the air to be moved to 50 feet to give him the air needed to complete the double flip.

When he went to the top of the ramp for his final run in the Moto X Best Trick competition, the crowd stood on its feet in anticipation.

This wasn't just a high degree of difficulty, it was a high degree of risk.

As Pastrana told the EXPN website before the event: "The big deterrent is that if I don't land it, it's not going to be pretty."

Pastrana accelerated down the ramp, came off the limp, and yanked on the handlebars. His feet followed the bike over his head once and as he returned to the upright position near the peak of his flight, he yanked the handlebars again and did another revolution.

He came down solidly with both wheels on the landing area, then made his way to the top of that ramp. The crowd at Staples Center went crazy. They knew they'd just witnessed history.

Pastrana hopped off his bike and threw both hands in the air. He ran back down the hill and was mobbed by family, friends, and fellow competitors.

Blake Williams, the bronze medalist in the event, called it "the stupidest thing I've ever seen."

That's a compliment in X Games-speak. We'll call it the greatest feat in the Staples Center. No translation needed.

SHOULD L.A. HOST ANOTHER OLYMPIC GAMES?

 Mention the 1984 Olympics to anyone who was in Los Angeles at that time and they're likely to describe it as the best two weeks in the city's history.

The world came to visit, and Los Angeles played the gracious host by somehow providing smog-free weather and traffic-less freeways. The Olympic-inspired Los Angeles Arts Festival exposed local audiences to performers from around the globe. The memories are so golden that no one even bothers to mention how the Games themselves had watered-down competition because of an Eastern Bloc boycott.

The 1984 Summer Olympics turned a $215 million profit that funded local sports programs for years afterward. And since the last time the Olympics came to Los Angeles, the region has added major sports facilities such as Staples Center, the Honda Center, the Home Depot Center, and the Pyramid. Stick a new track inside the Coliseum and every venue would be in place, removing one of the major costs associated with hosting an Olympics.

So why would it be a bad idea for Los Angeles to be an Olympic city again?

It really comes down to one date: September 11, 2001.

Ever since terrorism struck on our home soil, putting on an Olympics has become less about staging a sporting event and more about protecting what has been described as a city coming to visit a city.

The security budget for the 1984 Olympics was $68 million. The budget for the Salt Lake City Winter Olympics in 2002—the first Olympics after 9/11—was $310 million. Keep in mind that Winter Olympics are much smaller scaled and have far fewer athletes to protect than the Summer Olympics. The security tab for the 2004 Summer Olympics in Athens, Greece, was $1.5 billion.

In Athens there were aerial surveillance blimps, "sniffers" to detect chemical weapons, and a high-tech network that could scan faces and trace cellular phone calls. NATO provided air support and a naval fleet.

Instead of taking on the air of a joyous festival, Olympic cities can feel like a police state. Before the 2004 Games, American sportswriters were given gas masks and trained for terrorism disaster scenarios.

The good news is that no incidents took place. The last terrorist-related Olympic moment came before 2001, when a backpack loaded with explosives detonated in Centennial Olympic Park in the middle of Atlanta, killing one woman and injuring 100 people.

The bad news is budgets still have to be drawn up on the basis of the worst possible scenario.

Which brings us to the most logical argument against the Olympics: Why spend billions of dollars to protect the city for two weeks when that amount could be applied to protecting it year-round?

Aside from the security logistics, there's the reality of the changing landscape of Los Angeles. One reason the freeways were so clear in 1984 was people fled town because of fears of apocalyptic traffic jams. Now people are so event- and appearance-obsessed they would want to stick around to see what they missed in 1984.

In the past two decades, the population of Los Angeles has grown to 10 million. It's expected to grow to almost 13 million by 2020, which is the earliest available year in which Los Angeles could host the Olympics.

In 2007, Chicago won the contest to become the United States' nominee to host the 2016 Olympics, beating out finalist Los Angeles.

Maybe Los Angeles should consider itself lucky.

OFF THE FIELD

WHAT WAS THE BEST L.A. TEAM PORTRAYED IN THE MOVIES?

For all of the great teams in Hollywood's backyard, Los Angeles rarely fares well on the big screen. For example, in *Sports Illustrated's* list of the 50 greatest sports movies, the only example of Los Angeles was the misfit Little Leaguers whipped into shape in *The Bad News Bears*.

Maybe the movie studios think that Los Angeles has enough success in real life, so there's no way Middle America would drive to the theaters to watch more L.A. championships at the movies. Or maybe the movies require more of a stretch, a true suspension of disbelief, something like the Cleveland Indians winning in *Major League.*

Sure, Los Angeles could claim the fictional Western University of *Blue Chips*, as some exterior shots were filmed on USC's campus. But even though the team won the national championship, afterward a guilt-ridden coach, played by Nick Nolte, felt the need to confess the recruiting violations he had committed to assemble the talented squad that included Shaquille O'Neal and

Anfernee Hardaway. (Subtract serious reality points for the sportswriter played by Ed O'Neill, who smirked as Nolte spilled his guts. A true reporter would be angry that the investigative story he had worked on for months was just blabbed to everyone. So much for the big scoop.)

One of the most talented squads L.A. put together on film was the Lakers-like Los Angeles basketball team in *The Fish That Saved Pittsburgh*. It boasted Kareem Abdul-Jabbar, Norm Nixon, Connie Hawkins, and Lou Hudson. They also made one of the coolest pregame entrances ever seen on the big screen, emerging through a tunnel of smoke and lasers. But they were outdone when the roof to the Pittsburgh Arena opened up and the Pisces descended from the sky in a hot air balloon. Then they were outplayed by the Pisces for the championship.

Runner-up just won't do in Los Angeles.

Even *Angels in the Outfield*, the story of a boy, his father, and the California Angels, didn't end with a championship parade in Southern California. A slacker dad tells his son that they can be a real family again if the struggling Angels win the division. The boy prays for it to happen, and suddenly, with some heavenly help, the Angels turn into winners. But it climaxes with the Angels beating out the Chicago White Sox to win the division. Take about your low level of expectations.

That's why L.A.'s greatest on-screen sports team accomplishment came in 1978's *Heaven Can Wait*. It does involve angels (the lowercase, non-baseball kind), although it stars the Rams. Warren Beatty's character, Joe Pendleton, a backup quarterback, is taken to heaven by an overeager angel after an automobile accident...but it turns out Pendleton wasn't supposed to die yet. Since his body was cremated, he has to find a new set of flesh and bones to inhabit.

They settle on a recently murdered millionaire, Leo Farnsworth. As Farnsworth, Pendleton takes advantage of his wealth to buy the Rams and make himself the quarterback. And Pendleton/Farnsworth leads the Rams to victory in the Super Bowl.

At the time, the Rams winning a Super Bowl seemed more farfetched than a person coming back to inhabit a dead man's body. But the next year the real-life Rams actually made it to the Super Bowl, where they lost a closely contested game to the Pittsburgh Steelers.

Right now, just having a movie about a football team in Los Angeles would be fantastic enough.

WHAT'S THE BEST STADIUM DINING EXPERIENCE IN L.A.?

Buy me some peanuts and Cracker Jack? Please. These days at the ballpark you're more likely to find roast beef au jus, with a side of asparagus and garlic mashed potatoes.

As stadiums went upscale and catered to the luxury and premium suites instead of the bleacher crowds, the menu items naturally followed suit.

You could say the Angels started it, introducing the Diamond Club behind home plate when their renovated ballpark opened in 1998. It was so impressive that in his first visit to the revamped stadium, Cal Ripken, Jr. left the field during batting practice and walked up into the stands to check it out.

Then Staples Center opened, with its Arena Club, positioned halfway up the stands and open to the arena, so diners could watch the games below as they ate.

Suddenly a new sound was added to the traditional background noise of wooden bats hitting balls and sneakers squeaking on the court: the clanking of silverware on china. And now there was an alternative to the usual, watery overpriced ballpark beer: overly expensive wine.

There was one benefit to the chic cuisine: the Staples Center dessert cart.

This wasn't for the masses. It was more the province of the privileged few in the suites. But the whole mobility aspect somehow brings back memories of the days when hearing the ice cream truck's bells would send kids scurrying out of apartments.

Instead of Push-up bars and Popsicles, the Staples Center dessert cart features lavish chocolate cakes, "Snickers" cakes topped with caramel and peanut butter, liqueurs in chocolate shot glasses, and softball-sized caramel apples without a single brown spot inside.

The Staples Center cart helped make up for the drastic drop-off in stadium dessert options when the Dodgers ditched the beloved Cool-A-Coo in favor of the inferior "It's It" ice cream cookie sandwich. At Staples, dessert wasn't an afterthought, it was a highlight.

Still, something isn't quite right about the concept of eating cheesecake while seated on a plush chair in a wood-paneled room far from the action.

One of the best parts of going to a ball game is being able to toss your peanut shells and leave your trash on the ground without having your upbringing and sanitary habits called into question.

To that end, it's the latest innovation at Dodger Stadium (one that, alas, came after the introduction of the posh

Dugout Club) that ranks as the best thing to happen to sports fans since the roving vendor: the all-you-can-eat right field pavilion.

Introduced in 2007, it's a brilliant concept. Thirty-five bucks ($40 if you buy the ticket on the day of the game) gets you a seat and all the hot dogs, nachos, peanuts, popcorn, and sodas your hands can carry and your stomach can digest. From 90 minutes before the first pitch through the first two hours of the game, have at it. (Beer costs extra.)

As freelance writer Norman Chad described the Dodgers' all-you-can-eat pavilion: "This is why people come to America, this is why people stay in America."

Eating at a ballpark should be a unique experience unto itself, not something that attempts to mimic the latest restaurant in Beverly Hills. Besides...have you ever heard one person complain at an all-you-can-eat buffet?

WHICH STADIUM PROVIDES THE BEST LIVE EXPERIENCE?

90 As much as it costs to take your family to a game these days, the stadiums better make it worthwhile. This is one place where Los Angeles comes up short.

It's a strange mix of buildings that are either too old (the Coliseum and the Rose Bowl), too expensive (Staples Center), or too nondescript (Honda Center).

True to the car-crazy city's nature, most are difficult to access by public transportation. Even the most well-intentioned, eco-friendly fan will face a frustrating mix of rail transfers, shuttle buses, and hikes to get to Dodger Stadium or the Rose Bowl. And even the venues that are close to a rail stop, such as Staples Center and Angel Stadium, aren't close to housing centers. Their convenience gets negated by the distance.

But isn't Los Angeles a series of compromises? We put up with smog and earthquakes for the weather. It's a place of personal space and individual houses, not crammed skyscrapers; that just means more driving and traffic. Live in the hills for the beautiful views and risk fires and mudslides.

So it is with the far-from-perfect stadiums—and here's how we rank them

3. STAPLES CENTER

Or, more accurately, "$taples ¢enter." You can enjoy yourself there, but it's gonna be costly. The most popular tenant, the Lakers, have the most expensive tickets in the NBA. Even if you're going to watch the Kings, Clippers, Sparks, or Avengers, you'll pay a lot to eat and park. Did we mention parking? There weren't many convenient spots to begin with and the two biggest and closest lots now are occupied by the L.A. Live mega-entertainment and housing project.

The good news is, with the upscale restaurant, private clubs, and luxury suites, there's no better place in town to watch a game in high style. But the average folks are treated like an afterthought, stuck far away from the action above the three decks of suites, not even allowed to share the same escalators as the better-off.

Just about every seat in the lower bowl is good. But in no other building is the separation between the haves and have-nots as great.

2. DODGER STADIUM

After dealing with the traffic and the parking, fans are treated to the best visual reward in town: Dodger Stadium in all of its beauty. From its perfect symmetry to the

233

distinctive zig-zag roofs over the pavilions (everywhere else they're just bleachers), it's a classic, a baseball palace, and it retains enough of its original feel that it's easy to imagine Sandy Koufax or Don Drysdale on the pitcher's mound, delivering to home plate.

Then again, classic is another way of saying aged. Dodger Stadium, which opened in 1962, is second only to Chicago's Wrigley Field in National League stadium seniority. Even though the Dodgers have added revenue-boosting premium seats and luxury boxes, they haven't found a way to make the concession stands larger and more efficient. You can miss two innings going to get food. Of course, the reward for the wait *is* a Dodger Dog.

And in recent years it's as if the troublemakers, with apparently nothing better to do, have started showing up at Dodger Stadium, bringing back memories of rowdy Raiders games at the Coliseum.

From a baseball purist's perspective, Dodger Stadium is a shrine. But novel baseball fans won't get it. They need more stimulation, and Dodger Stadium doesn't provide it.

1. ANGEL STADIUM

From the kids' play area to the dancing geysers behind center field, Angel Stadium has stimulation. Of course the other word people would use to describe the place is "sterilization," with ushers determined to keep everyone in line and in their seats.

But keeping people in check means keeping the experience enjoyable for the majority of the fans, without the threats of fights breaking out.

And one thing Angels owner Arturo Moreno understood from the day he took over the team was less expenses means more happy fans. The typical cost to take a family of four to an Angels game is $40 less than a Dodgers game, according to Team Marketing Report. The big differences are in the cost of beer (which Moreno famously promised to lower at his introductory press conference) and the price of a cap. A cap? Sure, a small thing, but Moreno thinks it's a good idea to have fans wearing his team's cap. At a spring training game in his first year, he decided to give away caps on the spur of the moment.

True, Angel Stadium lacks a signature food item to rival the Dodger Dog. But overall, it provides a comfortable, entertaining environment (yes, that includes the mini-movie appearances of the Rally Monkey). Talk to women and kids and they'll tell you they prefer going to Angel Stadium. Given the intense competition for the entertainment dollar in L.A., those "swing voters" are too important to ignore. Their voices are winning out in this campaign.

WHAT WAS JIM MURRAY'S GREATEST COLUMN?

91

For 38 years, *Los Angeles Times* readers were blessed with the words of the greatest sports columnist who ever lived, the Pulitzer Prize-winning Jim Murray.

He redefined the craft, blending humor, Shakespearean references, and 20th century pop culture with a sharp insight into what made the games and the people who played them so fascinating.

He was the master of the simple, yet evocative lines. Michael Jordan was "as unstoppable as tomorrow." Rickey Henderson had "a strike zone the size of Hitler's heart." And there was this warning to what he considered the overly imperiled drivers at the Indianapolis 500: "Gentlemen, start your coffins."

Murray's first column appeared on February 12, 1961, and his last was in the paper on the day he died, August 16, 1998. Of the thousands he wrote in between, two emerged as the all-time classics: the July 1, 1979, column he wrote after he lost vision in his left eye, and the April 3, 1984, column after his first wife, Gerry, died.

In his ode to Gerry, he had you reaching for the Kleenex by the third paragraph, when he wrote, "I lost the sunshine and the roses, all right, the laughter in the other room. I lost the smile that lit up my life."

He recalled the details of her piano-playing skills, or the way she would leave notes for the kids if she was going to be gone for a few minutes.

At one point he apologized for straying from the usual subject, saying "I don't mean to inflict my grief on you, but she deserves to be known by anyone who knows me. She has a right to this space more than any athlete who ever lived. I would not be here if it weren't for her."

He certainly had a right to grieve in the forum he created.

But while the column was, per Murray's standards, exceptionally moving and well-done, it also reflected a common theme that stretched back to the beginning of the written word: the lamenting of a lost love.

What made the ode to his lost eye the definitive Murray column was the way, in relaying his sadness, it reminded us of his lyrical descriptions of the sporting world. That was his gift, the thing he did better than anyone else.

It also provided us with a personal scrapbook of his sporting memories. He saw Babe Ruth hit a home run when Murray was 12. He saw great base-runners from Willie Mays to Maury Wills.

At the same time it reminded us to appreciate the "common" sights we've all witnessed, and perhaps taken for granted: "the miracle of children, the beauty of a Pacific sunset, snowcapped mountains, faces on Christmas morning."

He described some of the sporting images he wished he could see again, including, "Rocky Marciano with his nose bleeding, behind on points and the other guy coming.

"I guess I would like to see Reggie Jackson with the count 3-and-2 and the series on the line, guessing fastball. I guess I'd like to see Rod Carew with men on first and second and no place to put him, and the pitcher wishing he were standing in the rain someplace, reluctant to let go of the ball."

Then he concluded, "Come to think of it, I'm lucky. I saw all of those things. I see them yet."

Actually, we were the lucky ones. We got to read what Jim Murray thought of them.

WHO IS THE MOST IMPORTANT PLAY-BY-PLAY ANNOUNCER IN L.A.?

92 We already know who the best announcer is. When the Dodgers moved to Los Angeles the city didn't just get a baseball team, it got the voice of Vin Scully, the best narrator the game has ever known, a Hall of Famer whose smooth, authoritative tone is as much a part of the Dodgers tradition as the color blue. It's all you need, which is why he doesn't share the booth with another announcer during broadcasts.

The truest sign of greatness is when rules change because of you. After Scully kept winning the Southern California Sports Broadcasters Association's Sportscaster of the Year award, the organization decided that no one could be declared the winner in back-to-back years.

There's no shortage of deserving broadcasters in this market who deserve to be recognized as well. Scully's Spanish-language counterpart, Jaime Jarrin, is a member of the baseball Hall of Fame himself. The play-by-play announcer for the Kings, Bob Miller, is a member of the hockey Hall of Fame and considered the best in his sport as well.

They're all great, but none of them is as important as Chick Hearn.

If we have already anointed the Lakers as the No. 1 team in town, then we must acknowledge the man who helped them reach the top of the podium, the man who made them relevant in the first place.

Even though the Lakers brought Elgin Baylor with them when they moved from Minnesota in 1960, even though they added Jerry West their first season in Los Angeles, and even though they reached the championship round in their second season here, they still drew crowds of less than 9,000 per game during their first four years in Los Angeles.

Jim Murray reminisced in his column about the time the Lakers attracted a crowd of 2,800 to the Sports Arena—*for a playoff game*. The Lakers went to St. Louis for the next game. Hearn, who picked up a few Lakers games when he wasn't broadcasting USC basketball games, did the broadcast. When the Lakers returned, there were 15,000 fans at the next game.

The Lakers made Hearn their full-time broadcaster. And we do mean full-time. He worked every game from November 21, 1965, through December 16, 2001. And somewhere along the way, his life's passion became the city's passion.

"Before Chick, basketball broadcasts were just more interesting than test patterns...Chick made it seem like World War III," Murray wrote.

Hearn managed to capture the fast pace of the game, his words keeping up with every dribble and pass. He coined so many phrases, from *slam dunk* to *airball*, it's now impossible to imagine a time when the basketball lexicon didn't include them.

Tuning in to a Chick Hearn broadcast was also an educational experience. In that automatic-weapon delivery of his, he informed listeners that the dimensions of the court were 94 feet by 50 feet, that the team that wins the opening tipoff also gets the ball to start the fourth quarter, and delivered other tidbits about NBA rules throughout the game.

He also taught by example. If he could be so dedicated to his job that he broadcast 3,338 consecutive games, maybe we ought to listen to what he had to say, and the sport he was describing.

As the Lakers became bigger, Hearn's status was elevated. When he died in August of 2002, his funeral mass was attended by the governor, the mayor, and the archbishop, plus a long list of Lakers starters that included Elgin Baylor, Jerry West, Magic Johnson, Kareem Abdul-Jabbar, and Kobe Bryant.

But Hearn never lost touch with the common folks, either. If Scully was more presidential, kept away from the masses by both the stadium design and his own desire to stay out of the spotlight, Hearn was more of a regular guy. You could stop by his broadcast booth before a game. If you encountered him in a lobby, he was likely to stop and chat.

As a result, almost 20,000 people filed by his old perch at Staples Center when it was opened to the public.

When a man who didn't wear a jersey can attract enough people to fill a sports arena, that's impact.

DID AL CAMPANIS DESERVE TO BE FIRED FOR HIS "NIGHTLINE" COMMENTS?

It doesn't seem fair that a man who did far more good than bad, who was responsible for assembling four of the Los Angeles Dodgers' nine World Series teams, came to be defined by a few statements he made on one night.

Fair? No. But it was the move the Dodgers had to make.

April of 1987 was supposed to be a joyous time. ABC's respected *Nightline* program was celebrating the 40th anniversary of Jackie Robinson breaking the color line, and Al Campanis, who was Robinson's minor-league roommate, seemed like a logical guest to provide insight and perspective.

By 1987, Campanis was the Dodgers' vice president in charge of player personnel, a job he had held for 18 years. He oversaw the rise of the Garvey-Lopes-Russell-Cey infield, and put together a roster that went to the World Series four times, winning it all in 1981.

Campanis wasn't even supposed to be on the show that night, but Don Newcombe, Robinson's old teammate, missed a flight and couldn't make it. Campanis was a last-minute replacement. He took a seat on the field of Houston's Astrodome after the Dodgers played the Astros. He was hungry and tired, it was late, and here was the 70-year-old man, under the lights, in front of the camera, with no connection to the world beyond except an earpiece.

When *Nightline* host Ted Koppel asked about the dearth of black managers and executives in baseball, Campanis said it was because "they may not have some of the necessities to be, let's say, a field manager, or perhaps, a general manager. Why are black people not good swimmers? Because they don't have buoyancy."

The story exploded. People of all races were outraged. It was a fast-spreading fire, and it caught up with Campanis in only two days. Before the Dodgers had even finished their three-game series with the Astros, Campanis was let go.

Campanis had actually helped Robinson make the difficult transition 40 years earlier. And he had helped to start another wave of integration, the explosion of Latino ballplayers, with the signing of Fernando Valenzuela.

The irony was that Campanis wound up taking the hit for a baseball-wide failure to live up to Robinson's standards and expectations (indeed, some of Robinson's final public statements before his death in 1972 included a call for more black managers).

But how does one explain away the mind-set that led

Campanis to say what he did? Even if he didn't have malice in his heart, it showed ignorance in his head. Blacks lack buoyancy? Where did that come from?

If Campanis had a position of lesser responsibility, he could have kept his job. But because his duties specifically included hiring and firing—especially managers—every subsequent personnel move would be subject to additional scrutiny. How could anyone be confident he wouldn't bring prejudice into his final determinations? With those statements out there, broadcast over satellite, preserved on videotape, it would be too difficult to look at any moves he made that involved a minority as being objective.

For the Dodgers' sake, as much as his own, he would have to be fired.

WHICH LOS ANGELES ATHLETE MADE THE MOST SUCCESSFUL TRANSITION TO HOLLYWOOD?

Somewhere in their minds, it has to be part of the thought process of every athlete who comes to the city: Maybe there's an acting career in it for me when I'm done.

For those who play well enough, carry enough status, and impress the Hollywood power brokers sitting in the expensive seats, there's almost a guaranteed spot on the screen at least once. But playing a role credited as "himself" doesn't cut it here. We're looking for the people who showed some serious acting chops, who went on to a second career long and accomplished enough that kids might think of them only as an actor, without knowing they ever were professional athletes.

So there's no room on this list for Shaquille O'Neal (*Blue Chips, Steel,* and *Kazaam*), who realized he'd have a much better chance at winning an NBA championship than an Academy Award, if he'd only concentrate on playing basketball. And even though Kareem Abdul-Jabbar took on Bruce Lee in *Game of Death* and delivered a memorable cameo in *Airplane*, no one ever confused him with Denzel Washington.

Here are the nominees for best performance by a former Los Angeles athlete:

5. ROSEY GRIER

Perhaps the former Rams lineman didn't land the best acting jobs: a guest spot here on *I Dream of Jeannie*, a guest spot there on *The Love Boat*, hardly ever a recurring role. But you could make the argument no actor has ever had a greater list of character names than Grier's: Bobo Johnson in *McMillan & Wife*, Salathiel Harris in *Kojak*, Big Slew Johnson in *Roots: The Next Generations*, Victor Hale in *The Glove*, and Powerhouse Watson in *The Jeffersons*.

4. FRED DRYER

The former Rams defensive lineman was a two-time Pro Bowler who had the distinction of becoming the first NFL player to record two safeties in a single game. He played in Super Bowl XIV, when the Rams lost to the Pittsburgh Steelers in 1980, and retired following the 1981 season.

He made his movie debut as a background football player in *Gus*, the 1976 movie about a field goal-kicking mule. But he got steady, serious acting work not long after he retired, and in 1984 he landed the lead role in *Hunter*, about a homicide investigator for the Los Angeles Police Department. He also showed up everywhere from *Laverne and Shirley* to *Cheers*.

3. MIKE WARREN

A member of two of John Wooden's national championship teams at UCLA, Warren made appearances on such 1970s hit shows as *The Mod Squad, Marcus Welby, M.D., Adam 12,* and *S.W.A.T.,* in addition to a role on the soap opera *Days of Our Lives* and in the film *Cleopatra Jones.* But his most memorable role was his Emmy-nominated turn as Officer Bobby Hill in the breakthrough 1980s police drama *Hill Street Blues.*

In 2007 he was still getting TV work, and his son, Cash Warren, was engaged to Jessica Alba. Can't get much more Hollywood than that.

2. MERLIN OLSEN

Talk about a career transition: Olsen went from being one of the Rams' "Fearsome Foursome" defensive linemen to playing the cuddly Father Murphy.

Olsen's career didn't stretch out as long as Dryer's or Warren's, but he was a regular on one of the biggest shows of the 1970s—*Little House on the Prairie*—in addition to starring in two of his own shows in the 1980s, *Father Murphy* and *Aaron's Way.*

1. ARNOLD SCHWARZENEGGER

Maybe it's because he never lost the accent that you don't think of him as a Los Angeles athlete, but he did move to Cal-ee-forn-ee-ya in 1968, and he won the Mr. Olympia bodybuilding competition six times afterward. He was working out in Gold's Gym in Venice while they shot the documentary *Pumping Iron*, which made him a star.

So maybe most of his roles don't involve long soliloquies, and it should be noted that his greatest character was a cyborg killing machine. But he has appeared in 30 movies that have grossed a total of more than $1.6 billion in the box office.

And he even landed a role as the governor.

WHICH L.A. SPORTS FIGURE WOULD BE MOST USEFUL IN A "SIX DEGREES OF SEPARATION" GAME?

You know the "Six Degrees" game, right? It started as a way to prove the ubiquity of Kevin Bacon, and showed it's possible to link him to practically any actor in cinematic history within six steps.

Of all the L.A. sports figures, Bill Sharman would have to be the Kevin Baconiest.

At first it sounds ridiculous to link someone who spent his playing career with the Boston Celtics with anything associated with Los Angeles. But Sharman defies easy categorization.

Even calling him a Hall of Famer isn't specific enough, since he's been enshrined in the basketball Hall of Fame as both a player and coach. (John Wooden and Lenny Wilkens are the only two other men doubly honored.)

Sharman went to USC, overlapping one year with Tex Winter. Winter has coached for some 60 years, including an assistant's role with Phil Jackson during the Chicago

Bulls dynasty. Right there that bridges you to Michael Jordan, Scottie Pippen, and the 1990s Bulls, not to mention all the different doors opened by Winter's coaching stints at Marquette, Northwestern, Washington, the Houston Rockets, and Long Beach State.

Back to Sharman: He was one of the best-shooting guards during his 10 years in the league, and remains one of the 10 best free-throw shooters in NBA history (88 percent). He played with four Celtics championship teams with the likes of Bill Russell, Bob Cousy, Sam Jones, and K.C. Jones, before becoming a coach. He coached everywhere from Cal State Los Angeles to the ABA, where he won a championship coaching the Utah Stars. His glory days came when he coached the Lakers, starting with the 1971–72 team that won 69 games and brought the first NBA championship to Los Angeles. In that capacity, he coached Wilt Chamberlain, Jerry West, Gail Goodrich, Pat Riley, and, ever so briefly, Elgin Baylor. After coaching he moved on to the front office, where he has served as a general manager, president, or consultant (his current position) for three decades.

But what makes him even more valuable if you're trying to connect players across sports is that Sharman spent five years in the Brooklyn Dodgers' minor league system. He was called up to the big leagues in 1951 and was actually in the Dodgers' dugout when the Giants beat them on Bobby Thomson's "Shot Heard Round the World."

So thanks to Sharman, you could go from Jackie

251

Robinson to Dwyane Wade of the Miami Heat in six steps. Robinson played with Sharman, who coached Kareem Abdul-Jabbar, who played with Kurt Rambis, who played with Eddie Jones, who played with Wade. Two players, two sports, almost 60 years between their professional debuts, yet not that far apart thanks to Sharman.

WHAT WAS THE BEST SPORTS TV SHOW SET IN LOS ANGELES?

 96

The White Shadow, which ran on CBS from 1978–81, is the best sports television show set anywhere. That it happened to be in Los Angeles just made for richer, more believable storylines...not to mention a legitimate excuse to have a cameo appearance by Elgin Baylor.

Not that there was much competition from the other shows set in the city.

Hang Time was just like *Saved By the Bell*, and all of the other sanitized high school-themed knockoffs of *Beverly Hills 90210* that came along in the 1990s, only its key characters happened to play on the basketball team. The only thing that makes it relevant today is that NBA-player-turned-actor Reggie Theus, who played the coach, was hired as the coach of the Sacramento Kings in 2007. Imagine if Bob Uecker got a big-league manager's job after the *Mr. Belvedere* days.

HBO's *Arli$$* was about a conniving sports agent (is there any other kind) and landed big current sports stars for guest appearances. But the titular agent had no redeeming qualities; the show didn't have any *Jerry Maguire* emotional breakdowns or breakthroughs. Ultimately you didn't learn anything from *Arli$$.*

That same lack of repercussions plagued *1st & 10,* the look at the fictional California Bulls that ran on HBO during the 1980s. Players frolicked with groupies without fear of catching the AIDS virus. There was no concern about the toll the game—or the drugs it required to keep playing it—took on the players. The show did get points for promoting Coach T.D. Parker to become the league's first African American general manager. But those points are deducted, in retrospect, because that character was played by O. J. Simpson. Mostly, the show just took advantage of the extra leeway afforded by being on cable. Think of the gratuitous Bada Bing shots in *The Sopranos*, without any of the intense characters or moral decisions.

By contrast, *The White Shadow*, which revolved around a white former NBA player's job coaching a mostly black team, was filled with tough real-world choices, even though most of the main characters were high school students. The issues tackled on the show included alcoholism, drug use, gambling, and death. Even if sex wasn't graphically depicted, it was a topic and it wasn't treated frivolously. In one episode, the point guard wrestled with how to tell the center he had slept with his girlfriend...and potentially given her a venereal disease.

The show did have its lighter moments, including the

team's ill-fated attempt to launch a musical career, a visit from the Harlem Globetrotters, and a hilarious trip to the golf course.

The city served as a backdrop to it all, Los Angeles with all of its opportunities to make it big in showbiz, and all of its perils threatening to derail even the modest dream of graduating high school. Somehow the show made it all seem realistic, from the action on the court to the life on the streets.

SUPERLATIVES

WHO IS THE GREATEST SPORTING ICON TO PLAY IN L.A.?

 To even be a candidate for this category, an athlete must be identifiable by one name only. Koufax. Wilt. Magic. Kareem. Reggie. But there's one name that tops them all.

Gretzky.

No other athlete who came through the city is as singularly identified with his sport as Wayne Gretzky. Ask anyone with even the slightest knowledge of the sport to name a hockey player off the top of his head, chances are it's Gretzky.

If the Los Angeles Kings didn't get him at his peak, they at least had him in his prime.

In 1988–89, his debut season with the Kings, he had 168 points. It might not have ranked among his top six scoring seasons, but it did surpass his average of 163 points during his nine NHL seasons with the Edmonton Oilers.

Gretzky won all four of his Stanley Cup championships with the Oilers, and that's where his legend was formed. Still, his days in Los Angeles are a major part of the Gretzky story.

Showing his flair for the dramatic, he scored a goal on his first shot as a King. And he was wearing a Kings jersey when he broke Gordie Howe's record for most career points.

Gretzky couldn't be considered rental furniture, like some of the other icons that came through town.

Yes, the Angels got 39 home runs from Reggie Jackson—a higher number than all but one of his seasons in New York—when he came to Anaheim in 1982. But honestly, the only time you'd think of Jackson in an Angels uniform instead of Yankee pinstripes is if you're talking about his cameo in *The Naked Gun*.

Kareem Abdul-Jabbar, the NBA's all-time leading scorer, wasn't enough of a salesman to represent the sport. The man he succeeded in the line of great Lakers centers, Wilt Chamberlain, stayed in Los Angeles after his playing days ended. But at his peak he had to share top billing—and was usually beaten by—Bill Russell. Magic Johnson also had a doppelganger in Larry Bird, before giving way to Michael Jordan.

Jerry West? We're talking icon, not logo. There is a difference.

The biggest name to play for the Rams was Joe Namath, but this was a beat-up, broken-down version, not Broadway Joe. Namath appeared in only four games and threw three touchdowns for the Rams in 1977.

Eric Dickerson set the single-season rushing record as a Ram, with 2,105 yards in 1984. But most people would still put the previous record-holder, O. J. Simpson, ahead of Dickerson on the all-time list. And both would trail Jim Brown.

Besides, no one wants to engage Gretzky in battle on the basis of records. Gretzky held 61 NHL records upon his retirement. All they had to do for the NHL record book is to keep pasting Gretzky's name again and again.

The final argument in Gretzky's favor is that definitive nickname: The Great One. There's only person who answers to that moniker. Now that's iconic.

IF YOU COULD ATTEND ONE EVENT IN L.A. SPORTS HISTORY, WHAT WOULD IT BE?

98 Imagine you had a time machine, a good ticket broker, and recurring amnesia. You could travel to any date, go see any event, and immediately forget why you were there, so the action would seem fresh. The one restriction: You could only go to events in the Los Angeles region.

If being there for the championship moment mattered most to you, you could catch the Angels winning the World Series, or the Ducks winning the Stanley Cup, but only one of the Dodgers' five World Series victories (1963) would be eligible. You could attend five of the Lakers' nine championship-clinching games, but you couldn't see Magic Johnson's 42-point performance in 1980.

Would you go to the first Super Bowl? If so, you'd be disappointed to find it wasn't the mega-event it is today. In fact, it wasn't even called the Super Bowl; it was the first World Championship Game between the AFL and NFL. Only 61,946 people showed up, leaving one third of the Coliseum empty.

None of the Super Bowls played in the Coliseum or Rose Bowl was a classic. The closest was Miami's 14–7 victory over Washington in Super Bowl VII, but Washington's only touchdown came on a fumble return from Miami kicker Garo Yepremian's famous flubbed pass.

Watching Mary Lou Retton vault her way to a perfect 10 score, a Gold Medal, and instant fame at the 1984 Olympics gymnastics competition would be fun.

The problem is that the whole vault, from the time she takes off down the runway, hits the board, and does a backward somersault, a full twist, and a rock-solid landing, takes only five seconds. Is it worth it to travel back through two decades just to watch five seconds?

What the Retton vault did capture was the unpredictable aspect of sports, the out-of-nowhere moments that we hope for every time we buy a ticket. A championship game doesn't come as a surprise. It's scheduled. The trophy is in the building, ready to be handed out.

Sports are better when something is delivered without a promise, when something goes from remote possibility to reality.

That's why the place to be was Dodger Stadium on September 9, 1965: Sandy Koufax on the mound against the Chicago Cubs.

He already had pitched three no-hitters in his career, so yes, there was a possibility that he could hold the Cubs without a hit. But he did it one better. He kept them off the bases completely, throwing the eighth perfect game in Major League Baseball history.

How often do you get to see a legend outperform even his own lofty standards? Koufax was masterful that game, with a sharp curveball and a stronger-than-usual fastball. He struck out 14 batters, including the final six.

By the way, Cubs pitcher Bob Hundley allowed only one hit that day, with the Dodgers' lone run coming on an error. It was the epitome of a pitching duel.

Another benefit of being there: exclusivity. Only 29,131 fans were at the Stadium that day (or as Vin Scully described the atmosphere in the tense ninth inning: "29,000 people in the ballpark...and a million butterflies.")

But after the final strikeout, the delirious fans sounded like a sellout crowd celebrating a championship. They came to watch a baseball game, and witnessed history.

WHO IS THE GREATEST ATHLETE FROM LOS ANGELES?

Whoever gets this award is emerging from a crowded field. In no particular order, there's Tiger Woods, John Elway, Eddie Murray, Oscar De La Hoya, Cheryl Miller, Bret Saberhagen, Tony Gwynn, Billie Jean King, Rafer Johnson, Lisa Leslie, and Darryl Strawberry, just to name a few.

But it's not worth going through the credentials of the other nominees. The winner has to be Jackie Robinson. No one can match his combination of athletic ability and historic impact.

Robinson was born in Georgia in 1919, but his family moved to Pasadena the next year. While at Pasadena's John Muir High, he excelled at baseball, football, basketball, and track. Oh, he also won a West Coast tennis tournament.

At UCLA he became the first man to letter in four sports. Robinson was the two-time leading scorer in the Southern Division of the Pacific Coast Conference (the fore-runner of the Pac-10) in basketball. In football he led the nation in punt return yardage twice. He leaped almost 25 feet to win the NCAA broad jump championship. Ironically, baseball was his worst sport at UCLA.

But baseball became the vehicle by which he made a living—and the means he used to change the country.

Robinson's career accomplishments—a .311 batting average, 947 runs scored, 734 RBI, and Rookie of the Year and MVP awards—would have been impressive enough just on their own. Knowing that he pulled them off under the unprecedented stress of being the first African American to play Major League Baseball, with the public animosity he faced from opponents and private dislike of some of his teammates, make the numbers seem, well, Ruthian.

Robinson deserves his own adjective, one that summarizes the class and dignity he displayed, the poise he had to maintain in order to keep the door open for the black ballplayers who hoped to follow him.

Given the chance, African Americans flourished. They went on to set baseball's career records for home runs, runs batted in, total bases, runs, stolen bases, and walks.

"If it hadn't have been for him, I know I wouldn't have been in the major leagues when I was—if ever," Hall of Famer Frank Robinson told mlb.com on the 60th anniversary of Jackie Robinson's first big-league game. "He paved the way for all of us that came after him because of the way he conducted himself and the way he played the game and the success that he had."

Robinson represents the way Los Angeles residents

would like to think of themselves: as tolerant, caring, and champions of an inclusive society. It's the version of the city that elected Tom Bradley mayor, not the one that burned after the Rodney King beating verdict came down.

Who better than Jackie Robinson to serve as an example of the best athlete—and citizen—Los Angeles is capable of producing?

WHO HAD THE GREATEST ATHLETIC CAREER IN LOS ANGELES?

100

You've made it all the way to the end, so we won't keep you in suspense any longer. There's only one athlete who played a critical role in two local dynasties. His name is Kareem Abdul-Jabbar, a critical member of the championship reigns of UCLA and the Lakers.

Well, technically his name was Lew Alcindor when he led UCLA to 3 of the 10 national championships during the John Wooden era. But there's no mistaking that lanky, 7-foot-2 body and the skyhook.

He still holds the school records for highest career scoring average (26.4 points per game) and most field goals (934, shared with Don Maclean). In 1966–67 he set single-season records for most points (870), highest scoring average (29.0), and most field goals (346). The 61 points he scored against Washington State on February 25, 1967, are the most by a Bruin and the most in Pauley Pavilion.

More important than all of those individual numbers was UCLA's record during his three varsity seasons: 88–2.

He went by Abdul-Jabbar by the time he got to the NBA's

Milwaukee Bucks, which is where he had his most dominant seasons (including averages of 34.8 points, 16.6 rebounds, and 4.6 assists in 1971–72.)

Milwaukee required four players from the Lakers to send Kareem to Los Angeles in 1975. In Los Angeles he won the league's MVP award three times and led the Lakers in scoring for 11 consecutive seasons.

Abdul-Jabbar didn't get the Lakers to the NBA finals during his first four seasons with the Lakers. Fortunes changed with the arrival of Magic Johnson in 1979. The knock against Abdul-Jabbar also carried a reverse twist. It was true that he never won a championship without playing alongside two of the NBA's all-time great guards: Johnson and Oscar Robertson (in Milwaukee). But neither of those great guards ever won a championship without Abdul-Jabbar.

If Magic was the smiling face of the Lakers in the 1980s, Abdul-Jabbar was the heart. He was the steady beat that kept the Lakers grounded at a regular pace and gave them a reliable scoring threat when the fast breaks slowed down and the easy baskets went away.

It's mystifying that Abdul-Jabbar isn't mentioned more often in discussion of the NBA's all-time great players. He meets the two main criteria we want to see from our basketball stars: winning and scoring. His six NBA championship rings are exceeded by only nine players in NBA history. His 38,387 points are exceeded by...no one.

Abdul-Jabbar is a jazz aficionado, and if the 1980s

Lakers were a be-bop band, he would be the bass, providing the steady background, with the occasional solo riff. But he never did much to call attention to himself.

The lingering image of Magic's first game as a Laker is the exuberant hug he wrapped around Kareem, a picture etched in our minds even more than Kareem's skyhook that won the game. And even though Johnson produced one of the all-time great NBA finals performances to win Game 6 and the championship in Abdul-Jabbar's absence in 1980, the Lakers would not have won Game 5 if Abdul-Jabbar had not played through a badly sprained ankle in the fourth quarter.

Jerry West scored more points as a Laker, but no Laker won more championships than Abdul-Jabbar. And no athlete in town is responsible for hanging more banners in arenas than Abdul-Jabbar. From Pauley Pavilion to Staples Center, in a city of winners he goes down as the ultimate.

SOURCES

The following books and resources were helpful during the research for this book:

- *The Anaheim Angels: A Complete History* by Ross Newhan
- *Rob Neyer's Big Book of Baseball Lineups* by (surprise!) Rob Neyer
- *UCLA vs. USC: 75 Years of the Greatest Rivalry in Sports* by Lonnie White
- *Fred Claire: My 30 Years in Dodger Blue* by Fred Claire and Steve Springer
- *Jim Murray: The Last of the Best* by Jim Murray
- *Madmen's Ball: The Inside Story of the Lakers' Dysfunctional Dynasties* by Mark Heisler

* The media guides and websites of the Angels, Clippers, Dodgers, Ducks, Kings, Lakers, UCLA, and USC

And if you ever need to settle a classic "Who Was Better" argument, the websites www.baseball-reference.com, profootballreference.com, and databasebasketball.com are invaluable.

INDEX
by Subject

G

Galaxy. *See* Los Angeles Galaxy
Game of Death (movie), 247
General manager decisions
    Clippers (best), 117–19
    Lakers (worst), 103–5
General Motors, 157
Gold's Gym (Venice), 249
Golden State Warriors, 100, 101–2, 108
Golf, 215–17
Green Bay Packers, 40–41
Group nicknames. *See* Team nicknames
Gus (movie), 247
Gutty Little Bruins, 69

H

Hang Time (television show), 253
Heaven Can Wait (movie), 227–28
Heisman Trophy winners, 173–75
Hill Street Blues (television show), 248
HIV/AIDS, 32
Hollywood Park, 7, 214
Home Depot Center, 10, 221
Honda Center, 221, 232
Houston Astros, 34, 165
Houston Oilers, 7
Hunter (television show), 247–48
Hurricane Katrina, 13

I

Indiana Pacers, 88–89, 101, 105
Indiana University, 172
Individual streaks, 43–47
"It's It" ice cream cookie sandwich, 230

J

"Joe Morgan Game," 54–55

K

Kansas City Chiefs, 32
Kings. *See* Los Angeles Kings

L

Lakers. *See* Los Angeles Lakers
Lake Show, 68
Last Season, The (Jackson), 94
Little House on the Prairie (television show), 248
Long Beach Armada of Los Angeles of California of the United States of North America Including Barrow, Alaska, 155
Long Beach Grand Prix, 214
Los Angeles, status as great sports town, 2–4
Los Angeles Angels of Anaheim, 155–57. *See also* Angels
Los Angeles Arts Festival, 221
Los Angeles Avengers, 114
Los Angeles Clippers
    attendance (2006), 3
    Brand, Elton, 114–15, 117–19
    fans, 20–21
    general manager moves, best, 117–19
    Lawler, Ralph, 115–16
    Los Angeles players, 27–28
    Miller, Andre, 27–28
    NBA drafts, 111–13
    Staples Center, 218
    Sterling, Donald, 120–22
    uniforms, retired, 114–16
Los Angeles Dodgers
    1988 season, 57, 58
    all-time team, 137–46
    announcers, 3–4, 239
    attendance (2006), 3
    Baseball Hall of Fame, 124–29
    "Beat L.A." chants, 25
    Campanis, Al, 243–45
    characters, greatest, 81–83

INDEX

by Name

R

Rambis, Kurt, 53, 252
Ratliff, Theo, 102
Rau, Doug, 133–34
Reed, Jody, 37
Reese, Pee Wee, 66, 124
Reiker, Rick, 60
Retton, Mary Lou, 262
Reuss, Jerry, 34, 82
Rigney, Bill, 167
Riley, Pat
    1988 playoffs, 57
    1989 playoffs, 77–79
    Lakers greatest coaches, 86
    Sharman, Bill, 251
    Showtime, 69
Ripken, Cal, Jr., 126, 229
Roberts, Dave, 125
Robertson, Oscar, 268
Robinson, Frank, 265
Robinson, Jackie
    Aaron, Henry, 76
    Baseball Hall of Fame, 124
    Campanis, Al, 243, 244
    Los Angeles athletes, greatest,
      264–66
    Roy Campanella Night, 65
    Sharman, Bill, 251–52
Robitaille, Luc, 202, 209
Rockne, Knute, 182
Rodman, Dennis, 83
Rodriguez, Alex, 126
Rodriguez, Francisco, 59, 166, 167
Rogers, Rodney, 119
Roseboro, Joe, 136
Roski, Ed, 8
Rozelle, Pete, 8
Russell, Bill (Celtics center), 53, 251, 259
Russell, Bill (Dodgers shortstop), 48–49, 139
Ruth, Babe, 237
Ryan, Nolan, 128, 165, 166

S

Saberhagen, Bret, 264
Salmon, Tim, 162, 164
Sampras, Pete, 43, 215–17
Samueli, Henry, 200
Sanchez, Luis, 151
Sax, Steve, 138, 146
Schembechler, Bo, 64
Schofield, Dick, 161
Schwarzenegger, Arnold, 249
Scioscia, Mike
    Angels manager, 159, 167
    NLCS (1988), 130–31, 146
    Piazza, Mike, 137
Scott, Byron, 78, 106
Scully, Vin, 4, 130, 239, 241, 263
Selanne, Teemu, 200, 205–6, 207
Sermons, Rodney, 182
Shackelford, Lynn, 51, 191
Sharman, Bill, 86, 250–52
Sheffield, Gary, 141–42, 150
Shelby, John, 130, 146
Sherman, Rod, 182
Simpson, O. J.
    1st & 10, 254
    Dickerson, Eric, 260
    Heisman Trophy, 173
    uniform number, 30–32
    USC-UCLA rivalry, 171, 172
Singh, Vijay, 216
Skinner, Brian, 117
Smith, Dean, 112
Smith, Kenny, 111, 112
Smith, Ozzie, 79
Snider, Duke, 124, 140
Soward, R. Jay, 170
Stanhouse, Don, 82
Stepien, Ted, 121
Sterling, Donald, 120–22
Stern, David, 62
Stewart, Tony, 213
Stiles, Bob, 69
Stockton, John, 111
Stoudemire, Amare, 111
Strawberry, Darryl, 26–27, 136, 264

ABOUT THE AUTHOR

Photo by Robert Gould

J.A. Adande is a columnist for ESPN.com and panelist on ESPN's *Around the Horn*.

Since receiving his bachelor's degree in journalism from Northwestern University, Adande has worked at the *Chicago Sun–Times*, the *Washington Post*, and spent a decade as a columnist at the *Los Angeles Times*. He lives in Santa Monica.

THE BEST SPORTS ARGUMENTS SERIES

The only thing better than watching sports is arguing about them...

Check out these other great sports books!

THE BEST BOSTON SPORTS ARGUMENTS
THE 100 MOST CONTROVERSIAL, DEBATABLE QUESTIONS FOR DIE-HARD BOSTON FANS
JIM CAPLE & STEVE BUCKLEY
Boston
978-1-4022-0822-5
$14.95 U.S.

THE BEST CHICAGO SPORTS ARGUMENTS
THE 100 MOST CONTROVERSIAL, DEBATABLE QUESTIONS FOR DIE-HARD CHICAGO FANS
JOHN "MOON" MULLIN
Chicago
978-1-4022-0821-8
$14.95 U.S.

THE BEST NEW YORK SPORTS ARGUMENTS
THE 100 MOST CONTROVERSIAL, DEBATABLE QUESTIONS FOR DIE-HARD NEW YORK FANS
PETER HANDRINOS
New York
978-1-4022-0823-2
$14.95 U.S.

THE BEST PITTSBURGH SPORTS ARGUMENTS
THE 100 MOST CONTROVERSIAL, DEBATABLE QUESTIONS FOR DIE-HARD FANS
JOHN MEHNO
Pittsburgh
978-1-4022-0967-3
$14.95 U.S.

THE BEST MINNESOTA SPORTS ARGUMENTS
THE 100 MOST CONTROVERSIAL, DEBATABLE QUESTIONS FOR DIE-HARD FANS
BOB SANSEVERE
Minnesota
978-1-4022-1061-7
$14.95 U.S.

THE BEST DALLAS-FT. WORTH SPORTS ARGUMENTS
THE 100 MOST CONTROVERSIAL, DEBATABLE QUESTIONS FOR DIE-HARD FANS
JAIME ARON
Dallas-Ft.Worth
978-1-4022-0966-6
$14.95 U.S.

THE BEST ST. LOUIS SPORTS ARGUMENTS
THE 100 MOST CONTROVERSIAL, DEBATABLE QUESTIONS FOR DIE-HARD FANS
BRYAN BURWELL
St. Louis
978-1-4022-1104-1
$14.95 U.S.

THE BEST LOS ANGELES SPORTS ARGUMENTS
THE 100 MOST CONTROVERSIAL, DEBATABLE QUESTIONS FOR DIE-HARD FANS
J.A. ADANDE
Los Angeles
978-1-4022-1106-5
$14.95 U.S.

THE BEST HOUSTON SPORTS ARGUMENTS
THE 100 MOST CONTROVERSIAL, DEBATABLE QUESTIONS FOR DIE-HARD FANS
JOSE DE JESUS ORTIZ
Houston
978-1-4022-1089-1
$14.95 U.S.

www.sourcebooks.com